Cambridge English: Proficiency 1

WITH ANSWERS

Authentic examination papers from Cambridge ESOL

CAMBRIDGE UNIVERSITY PRESS

CAMBRIDGE UNIVERSITY PRESS
Cambridge, New York, Melbourne, Madrid, Cape Town,
Singapore, São Paulo, Delhi, Mexico City

Cambridge University Press
The Edinburgh Building, Cambridge CB2 8RU, UK

www.cambridge.org
Information on this title: www.cambridge.org/9781107695047

© Cambridge University Press 2012

It is normally necessary for written permission for copying to be obtained in advance from a publisher. The candidate answer sheets at the back of this book are designed to be copied and distributed in class. The normal requirements are waived here and it is not necessary to write to Cambridge University Press for permission for an individual teacher to make copies for use within his or her own classroom. Only those pages which carry the wording '© UCLES 2012 Photocopiable' may be copied.

First published 2012
Reprinted 2013

Printed and bound in the United Kingdom by the MPG Books Group

A catalogue record for this publication is available from the British Library

ISBN 978-1-107-609532 Student's Book without answers
ISBN 978-1-107-695047 Student's Book with answers
ISBN 978-1-107-637467 Audio CD Set
ISBN 978-1-107-691643 Self-study Pack

Cambridge University Press has no responsibility for the persistence or accuracy of URLs for external or third-party internet websites referred to in this publication, and does not guarantee that any content on such websites is, or will remain, accurate or appropriate. Information regarding prices, travel timetables and other factual information given in this work is correct at the time of first printing but Cambridge University Press does not guarantee the accuracy of such information thereafter.

Contents

Thanks and acknowledgements *4*

Introduction *5*

Test 1   Reading and Use of English   *8*
         Writing   *20*
         Listening   *22*
         Speaking   *27*

Test 2   Reading and Use of English   *28*
         Writing   *40*
         Listening   *42*
         Speaking   *47*

Test 3   Reading and Use of English   *48*
         Writing   *60*
         Listening   *62*
         Speaking   *67*

Test 4   Reading and Use of English   *68*
         Writing   *80*
         Listening   *82*
         Speaking   *87*

Test 1   Speaking Test frames   *88*
Test 2   Speaking Test frames   *92*
Test 3   Speaking Test frames   *96*
Test 4   Speaking Test frames   *99*

Marks and results *102*

Test 1   Key and transcript   *124*
Test 2   Key and transcript   *132*
Test 3   Key and transcript   *141*
Test 4   Key and transcript   *151*

Sample answer sheets *159*

Visual materials for the Speaking test   *colour section*

Thanks and acknowledgements

The authors and publishers acknowledge the following sources of copyright material and are grateful for the permissions granted. While every effort has been made, it has not always been possible to identify the sources of all the material used, or to trace all copyright holders. If any omissions are brought to our notice, we will be happy to include the appropriate acknowledgements on reprinting.

Prospect Magazine for the text on p. 14 adapted from 'Oh tell me the truth about beauty' by Jonathan Rée, *Prospect* 1/3/09. Reproduced with permission; Tribune Media Services for the text on pp. 16–17 adapted from 'A Sunshade for the Planet' by David L Chandler, *New Scientist* 21/7/07. Copyright © 2007 Reed Business Information – UK. All rights reserved. Distributed by Tribune Media Services; Guardian News & Media Ltd for the text on p. 19 adapted from 'The Debutants' by Elizabeth Day, *The Observer* 16/1/11, for the text on p. 34 adapted from 'Inside IT' by Bobbie Johnson *The Guardian* 19/12/09, for the text on pp. 36–37 adapted from 'Frame at last' by Leo Benedictus, *The Guardian* 4/11/06, for the text on p. 50 adapted from 'Neologisms' by Henry Hitchings, *The Guardian* 5/2/11, for the text on p. 74 'Less is more' by Stuart Jeffries, *The Guardian* 11/2/11. Copyright © Guardian News & Media Ltd, 2011, 2009, 2006; The Management Lab for text on p. 39 adapted from 'Work-life balance' HYPERLINK "http://www.managementlab.org" www.managementlab.org. Reproduced with permission; Project for Public Spaces for the text on p. 54 adapted from 'Libraries that Matter' by Cynthia Nikitin and Josh Jackson. Copyright © PPS. Reproduced with permission; Telegraph Media Group for the text on pp. 56–57 adapted from 'A wet and wonderful ride in the wild' by Cameron Wilson, *The Telegraph* 4/1/04, for the text on pp. 76–77 adapted from 'Psychology: Just common sense?' by Aisling Irwin, *The Telegraph* 21/10/98. Copyright © Telegraph Media Group Limited, 2004, 1998; NI Syndication for the text on p. 59 adapted from 'Called to the barre' by Abigail Hoffman, *The Times* 24/1/04, for the text on p. 79 adapted from 'What is poetry?' by A A Gill, *Sunday Times* 8/3/09. Copyright © Times Newspapers Limited, 2004, 2009.

The publishers are grateful to the following for permission to include photographs:

Black & White Section:

p. 11 and 71: Thinkstock

Colour Section:

p. C2 (T): © DC Premiumstock/Alamy; p. C2 (B), C4 (TR), C5 (B) and C6 (B): Thinkstock; p. C3 (T): © NHPA/SuperStock; p. C3 (B): Image Source; p. C4 (TL): © Peter Phipp/Travelshots.com/Alamy; p. C4 (C): Getty Images/Ricky John Molloy; p. C4 (B): © Stuart Walker/Alamy; p. C5 (T): Getty Images/Zero Creatives; p. C6 (T): Sipa Press/Rex Features; p. C6 (C): iStockphoto/© Izabela Habur; p. C7 (T): Copyright Guardian News & Media Ltd 2011; p. C7 (B): © age fotostock/SuperStock; p. C8 (T): © Paul Rodriguez/ZUMA Press/Corbis; p. C8 (C): © Cn Boon/Alamy; p. C8 (B): © Frances Roberts/Alamy; p. C9 (T): iStockphoto/© Marcelo Piotti; p. C9 (B): Shutterstock/Specta.

The recordings which accompany this book were made at dsound, London.

Introduction

This collection of four complete practice tests comprises papers from the Cambridge English: Proficiency (CPE) examination; students can practise with these tests on their own or with the help of a teacher.

The CPE examination is part of a suite of general English examinations produced by Cambridge ESOL. This suite consists of five examinations that have similar characteristics but are designed for different levels of English language ability. Within the five levels, CPE is at Level C2 in the Council of Europe's *Common European Framework of Reference for Languages: Learning, teaching, assessment*. It has been accredited by Ofqual, the statutory regulatory authority in England, at Level 3 in the National Qualifications Framework. CPE is recognised by universities, employers, governments and other organisations around the world as proof of the ability to use English to function at the highest levels of academic and professional life.

Examination	Council of Europe Framework Level	UK National Qualifications Framework Level
Cambridge English: Proficiency *Certificate of Proficiency in English (CPE)*	C2	3
Cambridge English: Advanced *Certificate in Advanced English (CAE)*	C1	2
Cambridge English: First *First Certificate in English (FCE)*	B2	1
Cambridge English: Preliminary *Preliminary English Test (PET)*	B1	Entry 3
Cambridge English: Key *Key English Test (KET)*	A2	Entry 2

Further information

The information contained in this practice book is designed to be an overview of the exam. For a full description of all of the above exams including information about task types, testing focus and preparation, please see the relevant handbooks which can be obtained from Cambridge ESOL at the address below or from the website at: www.CambridgeESOL.org

University of Cambridge ESOL Examinations
1 Hills Road
Cambridge CB1 2EU
United Kingdom

Telephone: +44 1223 553355
Fax: +44 1223 460278
e-mail: ESOLHelpdesk@CambridgeESOL.org

Introduction

The structure of CPE: an overview

The CPE examination consists of four papers:

Reading and Use of English 1 hour 30 minutes
This paper consists of seven parts with 53 questions. For Parts 1 to 4, the test contains texts with accompanying grammar and vocabulary tasks, and discrete items with a grammar and vocabulary focus. For Parts 5 to 7, the test contains texts and accompanying reading comprehension tasks.

Writing 1 hour 30 minutes
This paper consists of two parts which carry equal marks. In Part 1, which is compulsory, candidates must write an essay with a discursive focus of between 240 and 280 words. The task requires candidates to summarise and evaluate the key ideas contained in two texts of approximately 100 words each.

In Part 2, there are five questions from which candidates must choose one to write about. The range of tasks from which questions may be drawn includes an article, a letter, a report, a review, and an essay (set text questions only). The last question (Question 5) is based on the set texts. These set texts remain on the list for two years. Look on the website, or contact the Cambridge ESOL Centre Exams Manager in your area for the up-to-date list of set texts. Question 5 has two options from which candidates choose one to write about. In this part, candidates write between 280 and 320 words.

Assessment is based on the Assessment Scales, comprising four subscales: Content, Communicative Achievement, Organisation, and Language.

Listening 40 minutes (approximately)
This paper consists of four parts with 30 questions. Each part contains a recorded text or texts and corresponding comprehension tasks. Each part is heard twice.

Speaking 16 minutes
The Speaking test consists of three parts. The standard test format is two candidates and two examiners. One examiner acts as interlocutor and manages the interaction either by asking questions or providing cues for the candidates. The other acts as assessor and does not join in the conversation. The test consists of short exchanges with the interlocutor, a collaborative task involving both candidates and an individual long turn followed by a three-way discussion.

Grading
The overall CPE grade is based on the total score gained in all four papers. All candidates receive a Statement of Results which includes a graphical profile of their performance in all four skills and Use of English. Certificates are given to

candidates who pass the examination with grade A, B or C. Candidates whose performance is below C2 level, but falls within Level C1, receive a Cambridge English certificate stating they have demonstrated ability at C1 level. Candidates whose performance falls below Level C1 do not receive a certificate.

For further information on grading and results, go to the website (see page 5).

Test 1

READING AND USE OF ENGLISH (1 hour 30 minutes)

Part 1

For questions **1–8**, read the text below and decide which answer (**A, B, C** or **D**) best fits each gap.

Mark your answers **on the separate answer sheet**.

There is an example at the beginning (**0**).

0   **A** radically   **B** centrally   **C** sweepingly   **D** rationally

| 0 | A | B | C | D |

The changing role of librarians

A combination of new technology and shifting student expectations is **(0)** ...A.... altering the job of a college or university librarian. Many librarians now regard themselves as information brokers who **(1)** .... and manage access to the information resources needed for learning, teaching and research. They agree that the pace of change has **(2)** .... and much more content is delivered electronically.

As a result of this, a librarian's responsibilities include information technology, knowledge management and institutional portals, in addition to being excellent managers and interpreters of services which may be provided from a growing **(3)** .... of global resources. Despite tremendous changes within library environments, these **(4)** .... are regarded as stimulating. Librarians respond by being flexible and adaptable in establishing a strong customer **(5)** ...., requiring the expansion of their skills to providing **(6)** .... to internet users and delivering e-services. **(7)** ...., most librarians say that many traditional library skills are still **(8)** .... in the digital world.

1 A enable   B facilitate   C incorporate   D render
2 A accelerated   B gathered   C raced   D hastened
3 A accumulation   B extent   C series   D range
4 A goals   B challenges   C achievements   D strengths
5 A point   B attention   C focus   D contact
6 A encouragement   B approval   C support   D supplies
7 A Moreover   B Nevertheless   C Similarly   D Therefore
8 A applicable   B expedient   C preferable   D parallel

Part 2

For questions **9–16**, read the text below and think of the word which best fits each space. Use only **one** word in each space. There is an example at the beginning (**0**). Write your answers **IN CAPITAL LETTERS** on the separate answer sheet.

Example: | 0 | N | O | T | H | I | N | G | | | | | | | | |

Why climb mountains?

There's **(0)** NOTHING more likely to irritate a mountaineer or explorer than to ask them why they do it, or why they are so willing to put **(9)** .... with danger and discomfort. In 1924 when George Mallory was asked why he wanted to climb Mount Everest, he replied: 'Because it's there.' It may be that, having been asked the same question several hundred times, Mallory just didn't care any more and this was the first phrase to **(10)** .... into his head. Then again, for **(11)** .... we know, it was simply his way of saying, 'Why not?'

This might seem self-evident **(12)** .... someone like Mallory. You climb Everest because you can. One way to look at people like mountaineers or explorers, or successful ones at any rate, is to see them **(13)** .... people who have realised what they are good at. When you read their books, more often than **(14)** .... they will come across as people who are **(15)** .... ease with their environment, **(16)** .... alien it might seem to an outsider.

Part 3

For questions **17–24**, read the text below. Use the word given in capitals at the end of some of the lines to form a word that fits in the space in the same line. There is an example at the beginning (**0**). Write your answers **IN CAPITAL LETTERS on the separate answer sheet**.

Example: | 0 | P | A | R | A | S | I | T | I | C | | | | | |

RAFFLESIA

Rafflesia is a rare (**0**) PARASITIC plant species found in Southeast Asia. *Rafflesia* has been (**17**) .... to a fungus because it lacks chlorophyll and is incapable of photosynthesis. Perhaps the only part of *Rafflesia* that is discernible as distinctly plant-like is the flower, which is said to be the world's largest. — **PARASITE** / **LIKE**

Many (**18**) .... have been keen to discover why the flower is so large, so they recently conducted (**19**) .... analysis on the plant. This resulted in the (**20**) .... that it has evolved almost 80 times from its origin as a tiny bud to today's seven-kilo mega-bloom. Although this (**21**) .... transformation took tens of millions of years, such an evolutionary spurt is still one of the most dramatic size changes ever reported. Such growth rates in humans would be (**22**) .... to us being 146 metres tall today. — **BOTANY** / **MOLECULE** / **REVEAL** / **ORDINARY** / **COMPARE**

The plant is also unusual in another way. Its smell is extremely (**23**) .... but this horrible trait attracts such pollinators as flies. It is thought that *Rafflesia's* huge flower helps radiate the smell over long (**24**) .... — **PLEASE** / **DISTANT**

Test 1

Part 4

For questions **25–30**, complete the second sentence so that it has a similar meaning to the first sentence, using the word given. **Do not change the word given.** You must use between **three** and **eight** words, including the word given. Here is an example (0).

Example:

0 Do you mind if I watch you while you paint?

   objection

   Do you ……………………………………………………… you while you paint?

0	have any objection to my watching

Write **only** the missing words **on the separate answer sheet**.

---

25 The thing I'd like most would be to visit the art gallery again.

   more

   There's ……………………………………………………… the art gallery again.

26 When I shouted at the boys to stop throwing stones they completely ignored me.

   took

   The boys ……………………………………………………… when I shouted at them to stop throwing stones.

27 What the lecturer said was not very clear at times.

   lack

   There ……………………………………………………… in what the lecturer said at times.

28 It was only when it got dark that Paolo decided to make his way back home.

fell

It was not ………………………………………… that Paolo decided to make his way back home.

29 The company avoids employing unqualified staff unless there is no alternative.

resort

Only ………………………………………… employ unqualified staff.

30 The careful preparation for the event ensured it was a memorable day for everyone who attended.

which

The care ………………………………………………… event ensured it was a memorable day for everyone.

Part 5

You are going to read a review of a recent book. For questions **31–36**, choose the answer (**A**, **B**, **C** or **D**) which you think fits best according to the text. Mark your answers **on the separate answer sheet**.

Joanna Knight reviews Roger Scruton's book 'Beauty'

Roger Scruton's new book 'Beauty' is a lucid and often graceful compendium of his reflections. He discusses beauty in nature and art, and above all in buildings. Even in an artistic paradise like the city of Venice, Scruton's attention moves quickly from the heroic buildings on the waterfronts to the 'modest neighbours' that surround them. 'Ravishing beauties,' he says, 'are less important in the aesthetics of architecture than those that create a soothing context, a continuous narrative as in a street or a square, where nothing stands out in particular.'

Beauty may have its roots in sensuous enjoyment, but even at its humblest it appeals to something larger: a willingness to consider, compare and arrive at a judgement. The 'judgement of taste', as the philosopher Immanuel Kant called it, spans two worlds: a private world of individual subjectivity, as idiosyncratic as you please, and a public world where you defend and develop your tastes through conscientious discussion – where you try to reason me out of wearing a yellow shirt, for instance, and I try to persuade you to get rid of the Carmen ringtone on your phone.

Scruton explores beauty in its various forms, starting with nature. He maintains, for instance, that the beauty of unspoilt wilderness depends on an evident absence of any fixed centre, a lack of prescribed edges. The beauty of birds, animals and flowers, on the other hand, is rooted in their existence as self-defining entities with boundaries of their own. And the special beauty of the human body belongs not to a mere assemblage of body parts but to the personality that finds expression in it. All this beauty gives you, as Scruton puts it, a sense that 'a world that makes room for such things makes room for you.'

Gardens are different again. They are places where wild nature has been disciplined, more or less sympathetically, into artificial forms. Their beauty is not that of infinite landscapes but of bounded spaces that surround us, rather like architectural interiors; and they enable Scruton to move smoothly from considering natural beauty to the far more contentious terrain of high art. Scruton can be as perceptive about sculpture, painting and classical music as about the varieties of natural beauty, but inevitably he is more controversial.

It is curious to observe how Scruton's feelings lead him to transgress his own standards of courtesy and decorum, and indeed of accurate and well-tuned prose. And you do not have to be a complete punk to suspect that the cause of his anguish may lie within him, and particularly in his premise that there is an unbroken continuum between the beauties of nature and works of art. Any attempt to cover the entire spectrum of reasonable pleasure with a single concept of beauty is bound, after all, to be quite a stretch.

Take the literary arts. Scruton is conspicuously vague when he invokes the concept of 'beautiful novels', and he sounds distinctly uneasy when describing story and dialogue as 'sensory features' of fiction, as if they could appeal to the same aesthetic sense as glorious sunsets. Yet, in the case of literature, beauty is only half the story, and this applies to other art forms too. In a revealing passage, Scruton confesses to a general dislike for cinema as an art form, but he makes one exception: you could take a still from any film by Ingmar Bergman, he says, frame it and hang it on your wall, and it would hold its own there like a picture. That may or may not be true; but single, silent images, however beautiful, are hardly a promising basis for understanding cinematic techniques or judging how they may have extended the ancient arts of storytelling.

Scruton sometimes reminds me of R G Collingwood, one of the most gifted philosophers of the 20th century, with a marvellous sense of history and, apart from a weakness for irritable sarcasm, a wonderful way with words. Like Scruton, he worked out his philosophical ideas in constant engagement with the arts. Unlike him, though, he was aware that there is more to art than beauty. In his autobiography, he described how he came to realise that works of art, however beautiful, will fail if they are unreal or imperceptive; and that works that disappoint lovers of beauty may still articulate issues about the world. If a work does not achieve beauty, it may still bear witness to truth.

31 In describing the buildings of Venice, Scruton reveals his belief that

  A they are less beautiful than some architects claim.
  B some of the streets lack anything of aesthetic value.
  C a harmonious whole is crucial in architecture.
  D beauty can be oppressive if it is overdone.

32 What point is being made in the third paragraph?

  A None of us should feel excluded from notions of beauty.
  B Physical beauty is no indication of character.
  C Observing wild creatures gives us a true sense of what beauty is.
  D Landscape is only beautiful if nothing man-made is visible.

33 The reviewer thinks Scruton's discussion of gardens

  A provides an opportunity for him to condemn artificiality.
  B allows him to emphasise the importance of discipline.
  C acts as a link between two different aspects of the broader topic.
  D balances the previous section on wild nature.

34 How can the reviewer's argument in the sixth paragraph best be summarised?

  A Including a section on works of art was a mistake.
  B The assumption about beauty underlying the book is flawed.
  C Scruton had difficulty fitting all his conflicting ideas on beauty into the book.
  D Scruton's normal writing style is inappropriate for a book of this type.

35 What is the reviewer's opinion of Scruton's section on the cinema?

  A The idea of displaying a still from a film is imaginative.
  B His coverage of film as an art form is inadequate.
  C He is right to concentrate on the beauty of Bergman's films.
  D Describing film as an extension of story-telling is exaggerated.

36 In the final paragraph, why does the reviewer refer to R G Collingwood?

  A to suggest that Scruton was not sufficiently involved in the arts
  B to point out the importance of taking history into account
  C to indicate how Scruton should have widened his view of art
  D to compare the two writers' fondness for sarcasm

Test 1

Part 6

You are going to read a magazine article about techno-solutions to global warming. Seven paragraphs have been removed from the extract. Choose from the paragraphs **A–H** the one which fits each gap (**37–43**). There is one extra paragraph which you do not need to use. Mark your answers **on the separate answer sheet**.

Cooling the Earth

As a last resort to combat global warming, researchers are investigating two possible ways of applying 'sunscreen' to the planet.

Even with the best will in the world, reducing our carbon emissions is not going to prevent global warming. It has become clear that even if we take the most drastic measures to curb emissions, the uncertainties in our climate models still leave open the possibility of extreme warming and rises in sea level. At the same time, resistance by governments and special interest groups makes it quite possible that the actions advocated by climate scientists might not be implemented soon enough. Is the game up in that case?

| 37 |

Quite recently a growing number of researchers have been taking a fresh look at large-scale 'geo-engineering' projects that might be used to counteract global warming. Basically the idea is to apply 'sunscreen' to the whole planet. It's controversial, but recent studies suggest there are ways to deflect just enough of the sunlight reaching the Earth's surface to counteract global warming. Climate models show that blocking just 1.8 per cent of the incident energy in the sun's rays would cancel out the warming effects produced by a doubling of carbon dioxide and other gases in the atmosphere. That could be crucial, because even the most stringent emissions-control measures being suggested would leave us with a doubling of carbon dioxide by the end of this century, and that would last for at least a century more.

| 38 |

There are two distinct proposals: reflecting away sunlight within the Earth's atmosphere, or blocking it in outer space. Each approach has its supporters and detractors. While tinkering with the atmosphere is likely to be much cheaper and simpler, space-based approaches may be longer-lasting and less likely to cause unwanted side effects – though they are much more technically challenging.

| 39 |

In addition, since it is naturally present at great heights above the earth, some researchers think an increase might not present as many unforeseen risks as some other suggested remedies for global warming, such as seeding the ocean with iron filings or other nutrients to encourage the growth of carbon-consuming organisms.

| 40 |

These drawbacks have driven others to look seriously at larger-scale, more expensive alternatives that might carry fewer risks. One that might do the trick is a space-based sunshade system. It may sound wildly implausible but some scientists are convinced that it is feasible.

| 41 |

These simple devices would be packed into metal containers in stacks of a million and propelled into space using electromagnetic rail guns – a method that has been tested in labs but never actually used. The acceleration is far too rapid for people or delicate equipment, but the method has long been proposed for shooting bulk material into space, such as water, rocket fuel or building materials. It could be cheaper and more reliable than traditional rockets.

| 42 |

Independent computer simulations show that the space sunshade could almost cancel out the temperature changes expected from global warming, except for a small area around each pole. That's because while greenhouse warming is uniform, the poles receive less sunlight than the tropics, so the effect of changes in sunlight is weakest at the poles. This regional difference

16

in cooling might cause unpredictable changes in weather patterns. And since the poles would see less of an effect from the dimming, they might still experience a significant loss of ice cover.

| 43 | |

Nobody wants to have to do this but if you get to the point where the alternative is six metres of sea-level rise, we might want to have this as an option. We're not going to implement it, but you certainly have to know what's possible. It's like emergency back-up surgery: you never want to do it, but you still have to practise it.

A The idea is to manufacture discs of silicon about 60 centimetres across. Each disc would be studded with holes of precisely calculated sizes, close to the wavelengths of visible light, which would scatter incoming light like a lens. The effect would be to produce a slight but imperceptible dimming of sunlight.

B So, is the concept of a technological fix new? Not at all; but while most remedies have focused on combating greenhouse gases themselves – finding ways to remove them from the air or scrub them from power-plant emissions – only recently have more radical ideas been taken seriously.

C Well, fortunately, if the worst comes to the worst, scientists still have a few tricks up their sleeves. For the most part they have strongly resisted discussing these options for fear of inviting a sense of complacency that might thwart efforts to tackle the root of the problem. Until now, that is.

D What's more, geo-engineering in general has major drawbacks. It does nothing about the carbon dioxide in the atmosphere, which would still produce effects such as ocean acidification. When carbonic acid runs into the oceans from rocks, they get more acidic. Nobody disputes that this will happen on an increasing scale. The only question is how much it matters to basic ecosystems.

E The simplest method put forward has been known for decades. That is to inject sulphur dioxide into the stratosphere, mimicking the cooling effects of volcanoes. Sulphur is cheap, and the means of releasing it could be as simple as pumping it up through a vertical pipe as much as ten kilometres long. Sulphur dioxide forms sulphate particles that are big enough to block part of the incoming sunlight, but small enough to allow infrared wavelengths – the heat radiation from the Earth – to escape back into space.

F So, which approach has the edge? It comes down to costs and feasibility. If we were suddenly faced with a climate catastrophe, the sulphur-particle approach is cheap enough to be essentially free. The engineering is simple enough that it could be put up in a couple of years. The space sunshade, though attractive, seems unlikely to be implemented. If cost were no object, one would want to use something like this latter scheme, because it's very clean and controllable, and would likely minimise any secondary effects. But it's very expensive. If you want to go to that much effort, it would be simpler just to change our energy systems.

G The approach is not without side-effects, however. Anything we do within the Earth's atmosphere might have unpredictable results that turn out to be worse than the cure, such as dramatic changes in regional rainfall or drought patterns, or chemical reactions that might disrupt ecosystems.

H Once launched, the receptacles would travel to the place between the Earth and sun where their gravitational fields cancel out, allowing objects to remain stationary relative to the two bodies. This is where the contents would be released. Scientists think they could be kept in place for 50 years or more.

Test 1

Part 7

You are going to read a magazine article about six young people who have been successful in various artistic fields. For questions **44–53**, choose from the people (**A–F**). The people may be chosen more than once. Mark your answers **on the separate answer sheet**.

Which of the successful young people

is inspired to investigate motivation?	44
is undaunted by the prospect of future demands?	45
makes a link between background and character?	46
appears to have thrived on negative feedback?	47
seems strangely unassuming given levels of success?	48
concentrates more on the medium than the message?	49
was prepared to make a leap into the unknown?	50
owes success to taking a step on impulse?	51
has a healthy disregard for adverse comment?	52
shows an understanding way beyond experience?	53

18

Six to watch

Sarah Carter chooses six young people to watch in various artistic fields.

A   Yasmin Shahmir – singer
'I was so excited. I felt euphoric,' says Yasmin having heard her first single being played. After five years spent DJing, this is one milestone the 22 year-old will never forget. The feline-eyed singer cuts a striking figure and you sense she was not destined to stay behind the decks forever. 'The song is about a time in my life when I was really going out on a limb – I'd quit my university course and moved to London where I was up for whatever life threw at me. At school I'd never been like the others – I'm half-Iranian, half-English and have a weird name. So I stood out a bit – maybe that's where my determined attitude comes from.'

B   Emma Hart – video artist
Emma Hart is tipped as 'one-to-watch'. Her output consists of video works, lectures and performances that challenge the way photographs and film are received. They make witty observations about everyday situations and ask the viewer to be active and questioning. 'The focus,' she says, 'is on how I use the camera, not on what I'm filming.' Recognition has been hard won. She worked first as a 'frustrated' office clerk. Bitten by the photography bug, she began a degree course but, constantly getting marked down on technical issues, dropped out. However, the criticism received was probably the making of her – it helped consolidate her artistic ideas, and made her more determined. It paid off in the end.

C   Danielle Hope – actor
'I'm 18, I'm a leading lady and a singer. I mean, who'd have thought it?' Danielle's life has undergone a considerable change – last year she was working as a waitress and thinking about applying to drama school. Instead, she auditioned on a whim and beat 9,000 hopefuls to win the lead role in a forthcoming musical. She seems remarkably unfazed by the task ahead. 'I don't want to let anyone down. It's self-pressure more than anything. Of course some will like my performance, some will hate it. Everyone's entitled to their opinion. I won't take it to heart – they won't be criticising me the person, but me the actress. It's all been so exciting – I've no idea what's going to be next.'

D   Eudon Choi – fashion designer
Eudon Choi trained as a menswear designer in South Korea and has always enjoyed the support of his family. After moving to London he won a prestigious award and his collection is soon to be stocked in 'Brown's Focus', an influential fashion boutique. For all the accolades, Eudon is surprisingly diffident. Is it a strain living up to all the hype? 'You can say that again.' For a relatively new designer, it's a great start. His inspiration comes from eclectic sources – he trawls vintage shops for military jackets and has, in the past, taken the aesthetic of the industrial revolution as his model. Now his clothes are acclaimed by fashion editors and worn by celebrities.

E   Andrew Sheridan – playwright
Andrew Sheridan's debut play is soon to open in Manchester. It has already been described as 'the best first play' by one of a group of leading young playwrights, the friends who initially pushed him into writing. It will be judged by the actors too, well known to Sheridan after a decade performing on stage and screen, and by his family. His family's reaction concerns him – none of them has ever had anything to do with the theatre and they haven't read his play. A desire to delve into 'what it is to be human' primarily drives his writing – 'what ultimately makes us tick.' Will his family find it all a bit weird?

F   Sunjeev Sahota – novelist
Sunjeev studied maths at university and didn't catch the reading bug until relatively late – he didn't read a novel until he was 18. Now, after eleven years spent 'catching-up', with his own first novel just published, he talks with the air of someone with a lifetime's reading behind him. It took him four years to write, working in the evenings and at weekends, but he didn't really expect to get it published – 'It was just maybe, maybe.' Now that it's out, he feels good. 'My friends aren't readers. They're just normal lads. But they've all bought the book. I'm anxious, slightly, and proud.'

Test 1

WRITING (1 hour 30 minutes)

Part 1

Read the two texts below.

Write an essay summarising and evaluating the key points from both texts. Use your own words throughout as far as possible, and include your own ideas in your answers.

Write your answer in **240–280** words.

1

The Effects of Music

We humans are a musical species no less than a linguistic one. This takes many different forms. All of us (with very few exceptions) can perceive music, harmony and rhythm. We integrate all of these using many different parts of the brain. And to this largely unconscious appreciation of music is added an often intense and profound emotional reaction. Shakespeare referred to music as the 'food of love', and for most people their lives would be the poorer without music. Music is capable of stimulating both passion and compassion, speaking to our very core and taking us to the heights and depths of emotion.

Music in Schools?

There is little doubt that regular exposure to music, and especially active participation in music, may stimulate development of other abilities. Some argue that music is as important educationally as reading or writing, and suggest that a musical education advantages those with mathematical aptitude. What people do not agree about, however, is which kind of music is the most educationally valuable. Some regard classical music as the only kind of music that should be taught in schools. However, leaving aside the problem of defining 'classical' in different cultural contexts, there is a strong case that all types of music are equally valid in stimulating an individual's potential.

Write your **essay**.

Part 2

Write an answer to **one** of the questions **2–5** in this part. Write your answer in **280–320** words in an appropriate style.

2   You have read an article in an international magazine on the topic of friendship. The magazine has asked readers to respond with their views. You decide to write a letter. In your letter you should briefly describe a special friendship that is important to you and assess the difficulties of maintaining friendships over time and in changing circumstances.

   Write your **letter**.

3   An English-language magazine has invited readers to send in reviews about a TV programme which has deepened their understanding of a particular country and its culture. You decide to send in a review of such a TV programme. You should briefly describe the programme and explain how it affected your views on the country and its culture.

   Write your **review**.

4   You work for the tourist office in your area. Your manager has asked you to write a report in English on a park that is popular with tourists. You should briefly describe the facilities that are currently available to visitors. Your report should also recommend two or three improvements that would enhance the park further and explain why these would attract even more visitors.

   Write your **report**.

5   Write an answer to **one** of the following two questions based on **one** of the titles below. Write **5(a)** or **5(b)** at the beginning of your answer.

   (a)   Marc Norman and Tom Stoppard: *Shakespeare in Love*
   An international magazine is planning a series of articles on love and marriage at different times in history. You decide to contribute an article on *Shakespeare in Love*. You should briefly describe Viola's relationships with Will and Wessex and explain how money and position in society influence the three characters' attitudes to love.

   Write your **article**.

   (b)   Philip K Dick: *Do Androids Dream of Electric Sheep?*
   'I want to have an animal; I keep trying to buy one. But on my salary…' Your tutor asks you to write an essay on the status of animals in *Do Androids Dream of Electric Sheep?*, evaluating the importance of real and electric animals to the society in which Rick lives. You should refer to events in the story to support your views.

   Write your **essay**.

Test 1

LISTENING (40 minutes approximately)

Part 1

You will hear three different extracts.

For questions **1–6**, choose the answer (**A**, **B** or **C**) which fits best according to what you hear. There are two questions for each extract.

Extract One

You hear two careers advisers discussing whether students should take a year off after graduation to go travelling.

1 When mentioning recent statistics on graduates taking gap years, the man reveals

   A his scepticism about the value of rushing to get a job after university.
   B his doubts about the validity of some research.
   C his understanding of the anxiety that prevents them from travelling.

2 What do the two careers advisers agree about a gap year?

   A Some employers consider it a lazy option.
   B The way graduates present it at interview is crucial.
   C Graduates should spend it doing something relevant to their career.

Extract Two

You hear a sociologist talking about consumer buying behaviour.

3 What does the sociologist say about the 'information search stage' of decision making?

   A It arouses a desire for a better situation.
   B It is likely to be incomplete.
   C It is a lengthy process.

4 According to the sociologist, how do marketing professionals most successfully influence people's choice of product?

   A They aim to create new aspirations in people.
   B They offer updated designs that increase customer satisfaction.
   C They improve websites to make buying their products easy.

Listening

Extract Three

You hear a man who has an internet company talking about selling goods online.

5   In the man's opinion, what is most needed when selling goods online?

    A   an appreciation of how it differs from shop-based selling
    B   a willingness to adapt quickly to new circumstances
    C   an awareness of how to make a website attractive

6   What is the man doing in answer to the interviewer's question about growing an online business?

    A   comparing the advantages of two business theories
    B   warning of the dangers of inadequate funding
    C   suggesting the use of external consultants

Test 1

Part 2

You will hear a student, Hannah Jorden, giving a short talk on the topic of soil.

For questions **7–15**, complete the sentences with a word or short phrase.

Hannah has found out that people have used soil as a **(7)** .... for thousands of years.

Hannah says that the increase in **(8)** .... is putting pressure on the way we use soil.

Pollutants from waste in the soil can enter the **(9)** .... and can affect both plants and humans.

Hannah has found evidence showing that waste pollution reduces the number of **(10)** .... in the soil.

The main cause of inorganic pollution is the **(11)** .... which takes place in many countries.

Hannah is interested in the fact that organic pollutants can directly affect the **(12)** .... in humans.

Hannah gives the example of **(13)** .... as a natural cause of acid rain.

Hannah has found that soil erosion caused by **(14)** .... has been of interest to the media.

Soil has become less fertile owing to the method known as **(15)** ....

Part 3

You will hear part of a discussion programme, in which a teacher called Simon and a business journalist called Trina are talking about the issue of change.

For questions **16–20**, choose the answer (**A**, **B**, **C** or **D**) which fits best according to what you hear.

16 What does Simon say about change when discussing linguistic expressions?

   A   It is an inevitable part of life.
   B   It is generally perceived as unwelcome.
   C   Its significance has altered over time.
   D   It brings improvements when they're least expected.

17 What do they agree about change in the business community?

   A   It is regarded as synonymous with progress.
   B   It is seen as unfortunate but necessary.
   C   It never seems to be questioned.
   D   It can lead to undesirable results.

18 What does Trina dislike about feedback forms?

   A   the scale of the reaction they can provoke
   B   the disharmony they can create within organisations
   C   the extent of their use in the world of education
   D   the justification they give to managers who want to introduce changes

19 When discussing day-to-day routines, Simon and Trina agree that people

   A   make too much fuss about small-scale changes.
   B   find that changes in the workplace mirror those in daily life.
   C   only like change that clearly benefits them personally.
   D   experience an ongoing cycle of resisting and accepting change.

20 In Simon's view, people will really enjoy an activity if

   A   they do it on a regular basis.
   B   they keep on changing it slightly.
   C   it represents a change for them.
   D   it coincides with their expectations.

Part 4

You will hear five short extracts in which people are talking about their involvement in award-winning projects related to the natural world.

TASK ONE

For questions **21–25**, choose from the list (**A–H**) what special feature of the project each speaker mentions.

TASK TWO

For questions **26–30**, choose from the list (**A–H**) what positive effect of receiving the award each speaker appreciated.

While you listen, you must complete both tasks.

A a combination of old and new methods

B the involvement of community leaders

C the recycling of local resources

D the adaptation of space technology

E an idea copied from another part of the world

F the use of a different material

G a method based on an accidental discovery

H the development of a single multi-purpose system

Speaker 1 □ 21
Speaker 2 □ 22
Speaker 3 □ 23
Speaker 4 □ 24
Speaker 5 □ 25

A Advanced technology was donated.

B The original idea was improved.

C Critics of the project were silenced.

D The attitude of local people changed.

E Related information could be shared.

F More staff were taken onto the project.

G Awareness of endangered species was increased.

H The economy of the region was developed.

Speaker 1 □ 26
Speaker 2 □ 27
Speaker 3 □ 28
Speaker 4 □ 29
Speaker 5 □ 30

SPEAKING (16 minutes)

There are two examiners. One (the interlocutor) conducts the test, providing you with the necessary materials and explaining what you have to do. The other examiner (the assessor) will be introduced to you, but then takes no further part in the interaction.

Part 1 (2 minutes)

The interlocutor first asks you and your partner a few questions which focus on information about yourselves.

Part 2 (4 minutes)

In this part of the test you and your partner are asked to talk together. The interlocutor places a set of pictures on the table in front of you. There may be only one picture in the set or as many as seven pictures. This stimulus provides the basis for a discussion. The interlocutor first asks an introductory question which focuses on two of the pictures (or in the case of a single picture, on aspects of the picture). After about a minute, the interlocutor gives you both a decision-making task based on the same set of pictures.

The pictures for Part 2 are on pages C2–C3 of the colour section.

Part 3 (10 minutes)

You are each given the opportunity to talk for two minutes, to comment after your partner has spoken and to take part in a more general discussion.

The interlocutor gives you a card with a question written on it and asks you to talk about it for two minutes. After you have spoken, the interlocutor asks you both another question related to the topic on the card, addressing your partner first. This procedure is repeated, so that your partner receives a card and speaks for two minutes and a follow-up question is asked.

Finally, the interlocutor asks some further questions, which leads to a discussion on a general theme related to the subjects already covered in Part 3.

The cards for Part 3 are on pages C10–C11 of the colour section.

Test 2

READING AND USE OF ENGLISH (1 hour 30 minutes)

Part 1

For questions **1–8**, read the text below and decide which answer (**A**, **B**, **C** or **D**) best fits each gap.

Mark your answers **on the separate answer sheet**.

There is an example at the beginning (**0**).

| 0 | **A** in particular | **B** in any case | **C** in turn | **D** in the end |

| 0 | A ■ | B ▫ | C ▫ | D ▫ |

Scientists and communication

Scientists are often accused of being poor communicators, yet there are many reasons why scientists, **(0)** ....A...., should be and often are good communicators. After all, science calls **(1)** .... enthusiasm and scientists often possess this **(2)** .... quality in large quantities. Enthusiasm can be infectious, but to command the interest of readers, scientists must develop their other **(3)** .... talents: clarity, observation and knowledge.

Those scientists who are logical thinkers can usually write clearly, and the more clearly thoughts are **(4)** .... , the greater their potential value. In the same way, those who observe must take account of subtle differences for the observations they may **(5)** .... as significant. Finally, those who write must have something of **(6)** .... value to say.

A scientist whose work never sees the **(7)** .... of day has achieved nothing of worth until somebody else hears about it. It is essential, therefore, for scientists to lay to **(8)** .... the myth that they cannot communicate, once and for all.

28

1 **A** on   **B** up   **C** for   **D** in
2 **A** arresting   **B** engaging   **C** catching   **D** fetching
3 **A** native   **B** innate   **C** standard   **D** typical
4 **A** put across   **B** come over   **C** given out   **D** set up
5 **A** document   **B** predict   **C** enter   **D** pronounce
6 **A** basic   **B** radical   **C** intrinsic   **D** central
7 **A** light   **B** start   **C** dawn   **D** birth
8 **A** sleep   **B** rest   **C** bed   **D** ground

Part 2

For questions **9–16**, read the text below and think of the word which best fits each space. Use only **one** word in each space. There is an example at the beginning (**0**). Write your answers **IN CAPITAL LETTERS on the separate answer sheet.**

Example: | 0 | O | F |

Film music

Any mention (**0**) ...OF... the movie Star Wars instantly triggers the resounding opening bars of the film score, which signals the presence of the enemy. But can you call to (**9**) .... who wrote the music?

(**10**) .... to the legendary film director Orson Wells, music accounts (**11**) .... half the work in a movie, mostly (**12**) .... the audience even knowing the composer's name. The cruellest (**13**) .... of it for the composer is that, in a good film, that is how it should be. If the art of dressing well is to all intents and purposes to dress in such a way that others do (**14**) .... notice your elegance, the art of a great music score is to fuse so perfectly with what is on the screen that audiences are unconsciously sucked (**15**) .... the mood of the movie. For this reason, even great movie music brings very (**16**) .... recognition to composers.

Part 3

For questions **17–24**, read the text below. Use the word given in capitals at the end of some of the lines to form a word that fits in the space in the same line. There is an example at the beginning (**0**). Write your answers **IN CAPITAL LETTERS on the separate answer sheet**.

Example: 0 B E A U T I F U L L Y

Extreme weather

Extreme Weather is packed with facts about the great forces of nature
and is a **(0)** ..BEAUTIFULLY.. illustrated science book by **BEAUTY**
the meteorologist, H. Michael Mogil. The aim of the book is to present
enough knowledge to understand the many **(17)** ……..... of the debate **COMPLEX**
about climate change.

Mogil is alarmed about the way the public has been **(18)** ……..... on this issue, **LEAD**
being pushed towards certain positions on climate change by the
campaigning of **(19)** ……..... and the news media's need for a good **POLITICS**
story. He wants to demonstrate that climate change is an **(20)** ……..... **CREDIBLE**
complicated issue, and that making overly simplistic **(21)** ……..... **ASSUME**
will inevitably **(22)** ……..... our understanding. He therefore **PAIR**
(23) ……..... emphasises that weather records are short, often **REPEAT**
incomplete and tricky to compare. Mogil suggests that, in the distant
past, changes in climate occurred in magnitudes far greater than in
recent times. It is the **(24)** ……..... detail with which these recent events **FINITE**
have been recorded that differentiates them from the past.

Test 2

Part 4

For questions **25–30**, complete the second sentence so that it has a similar meaning to the first sentence, using the word given. **Do not change the word given.** You must use between **three** and **eight** words, including the word given. Here is an example (**0**).

Example:

0 Do you mind if I watch you while you paint?

   objection

   Do you ………………………………………………… you while you paint?

| **0** | have any objection to my watching |

Write **only** the missing words **on the separate answer sheet**.

---

25 It can be difficult to make a decision when there is too much time to think.

   reach

   Having too much time to think may ………………………………………… a decision.

26 Visitors can only enter the exhibition if they have booked online.

   restricted

   Entrance ………………………………………… have booked online.

27 If Stevie hadn't acted promptly to put out the fire, there might have been more damage to the kitchen.

   in

   But ………………………………………… out the fire, there might have been more damage to the kitchen.

32

28 Taxes will most probably rise next year.

every

There ………………………………………………… next year.

29 Although she didn't agree with the management's decision, Chloe was forced to accept it.

choice

Much as she disagreed with it, Chloe …………………………………………. the management's decision.

30 We have taken to going to the cinema on Fridays.

habit

We …………………………………………………………… going to the cinema on Fridays.

Test 2

Part 5

You are going to read a newspaper article about young people and technology. For questions **31–36**, choose the answer (**A**, **B**, **C** or **D**) which you think fits best according to the text. Mark your answers **on the separate answer sheet**.

Young People and Technology

Danah Boyd is a specialist researcher looking at how young people use technology

If there's one cliche that really grates with Danah Boyd, who has made a career from studying the way younger people use the web, it's that of the digital native. 'There's nothing native about young people's engagement with technology,' she says, adamantly. She has little time for the widely held assumption that kids are innately more adept at coping with the web or negotiating the hurdles of digital life. 'Young people are learning about
line 5   the social world around them,' she says. 'Today that world has computer-mediated communications. Thus, in order to learn about their social world, they're learning about those things too. And they're leveraging that to work out the stuff that kids have always worked out: peer sociality, status, etc.'

It's no surprise she takes exception, really: as one of the first digital anthropologists to dig into the way people use social networking sites, Boyd has a track record of exposing the truths that underpin many of our assumptions about the online world. Along the way, she's gained insights into the social web – not just by conducting studies of how many kids were using social-networking sites, but by taking a closer look at what was going on.

Lately, her work has been about explaining new ways of interpreting the behaviour we see online, and understanding that the context of online activity is often more subtle than we first imagine. She outlined some examples at a recent conference in San Francisco, including the case of a young man from one of the poorest districts of Los Angeles who was applying to a prestigious American college. The applicant said he wanted to escape the influence of gangs and violence, but the admissions officer was appalled when he discovered that the boy's MySpace page was plastered with precisely the violent language and gang imagery he claimed to abhor. Why was he lying about his motivations, asked the university? 'He wasn't,' says Boyd: in his world, showing the right images online was a key part of surviving daily life.

Understanding what's happening online is especially pertinent while discussions rage about how perceptions of privacy are shifting – particularly the idea that today's teenagers have a vastly different approach to privacy from their predecessors. Instead, Boyd says, activities that strike adults as radically new are often more easily understood from the perspective of teenagers. 'Kids have always cared about privacy, it's just that their notions of privacy look very different from adult notions,' she says. 'Kids often don't have the kind of privacy adults assume they do. Adults, by and large, think of the home as a very private space. The thing is, for young people that's often not the case because they have little or no control over who has access to it, or under what conditions. As a result, the online world can feel more private because it feels like there's more control.'

This concept of control is central to Boyd's work, and it applies not only to
line 32 debunking myths about teenage behaviour, but also to similar ideas that have emerged about the rest of the web. Unlike some prognosticators who preach unstoppable revolution, Boyd suggests that control remains,
line 34 by and large, in the same places it always did. 'Technologists all go for the notion of "techno-utopia", the web as great democratiser,' she says. 'Sure, we've made creation and distribution more available to anyone, but at the same time we've made those things irrelevant. Now the commodity isn't distribution, it's attention – and guess what? We're not actually democratising the whole system – we're just shifting the way in which we discriminate.'

It's a call to arms that most academic researchers would tend to sidestep, but then Boyd admits to treading a fine line between academic and activist. After all, she adds, part of her purpose is to look at the very questions that make us feel uncomfortable. 'Part of it is that as a researcher, everybody's obsessed with Twitter and Facebook, and we've got amateur research all over the place,' she says. 'Plenty of scholars are jumping in and looking at very specific things. The questions I continue to want to ask are the things that are challenging to me: having to sit down and be forced to think about uncomfortable social stuff, and it's really hard to get my head around it, which means it's exactly what I should dive in and deal with.'

31 What point does Danah Boyd make about 'computer-mediated communications' (line 5)?

  A They set out to teach the young about social interaction.
  B They are an integral part of a young person's social interaction.
  C They act as a barrier to wider social interaction amongst young people.
  D They take the place of other sorts of social interaction for young people.

32 In the second paragraph, what do we learn about Danah's research into social networking sites?

  A It has largely sought to account for their rapid growth.
  B It has tended to question people's attitudes towards them.
  C It has taken the form of in-depth studies into how they are designed.
  D It has begun to investigate whether they are as influential as people think.

33 What point does Danah's example of the Los Angeles college applicant illustrate?

  A how easy it is to misinterpret an individual's online activity
  B how readily somebody's online activity can be investigated
  C what their online activity can tell us about a person's sincerity
  D how important it is to check the content of someone's online activity

34 The phrase 'debunking myths' (line 32) refers to Danah's view that

  A today's teenagers are less concerned about privacy than previous generations.
  B teenagers value the idea of privacy more in a domestic environment.
  C teenagers' attitudes to privacy are changing less than people think.
  D parents tend not to respect teenagers' need for online privacy.

35 Danah uses the term 'techno-utopia' (line 34) to underline her view that

  A her research has resonance for a community of web users of all ages.
  B people have unrealistic expectations about the influence of the web.
  C control of the web remains in much the same hands as before.
  D the web has a largely positive effect on many people's lives.

36 In the last paragraph, we are given the impression that Danah

  A feels that a lot of research about the web is lacking in sufficient detail.
  B is aware that some issues in her field cannot yet be researched fully.
  C regards herself as being more of a philosopher than a researcher.
  D is willing to take on research challenges others would avoid.

Test 2

Part 6

You are going to read an article about the work of a TV animator. Seven paragraphs have been removed from the extract. Choose from the paragraphs **A–H** the one which fits each gap **(37–43)**. There is one extra paragraph which you do not need to use. Mark your answers **on the separate answer sheet**.

An Animated Life

Adam Farish works in stop-motion animation – the technique of making TV cartoons by manipulating static models rather than using drawings or computers. It might sound a bit childish, but it isn't all child's play. 'I tell people what I do, and they go, "You can't do that. Get a proper job!"' A sheepish grin spreads across the face of Adam Farish, 36, who spends eight hours a day playing with dolls. 'It makes me laugh,' he shrugs. And, on cue, he laughs. It's an explosive, wheezy laugh, a brief eruption of permanently suppressed amusement. Even after three years as an animator, it seems as if he still can't believe his luck.

37

His company's big project at the moment is the new Rupert Bear series, *Follow the Magic*. Consequently, Farish has spent many months absorbed in Rupert's surreal existence. 'It is acting, but you're not using your own body to act with,' he explains. 'We come in and we have to pretend we're five-year-old toy bears rescuing elephants out of trees. It does something to your head after a while.'

38

This great mountain of work must all be performed to a minute level of detail, and with complete accuracy. If a character makes a large gesture, for instance, there must always be a slight recoil in the limb before they do it. This must be posed and photographed. Blinking, which a character must do all the time if it is to seem human, involves replacing an open eyelid with a half-closed eyelid and taking a picture, then replacing this with a three-quarter-closed eyelid and taking a picture, then switching to a fully closed one and taking a picture, then putting on the three-quarter one again …

39

When you factor in all the work done by others in building and lighting the sets correctly and providing each character with their props and costumes, it is easy to see why stop-motion animation has a reputation for being, well, slow. 'We've got a target of 13 seconds a day. Most other companies do three or four, but because we're doing series work and there's tight deadlines, we have to push it to 13 seconds – that is 325 frames in other words. It's quite strange,' he muses, 'because it's so … ,' he searches for the right word, 'dull.'

40

So, as far as anyone can tell, the knack of getting it right is handed out at birth, and not to many people. Yet despite the rareness of the skill, the animator's job is seldom secure. Most work on short-term contracts (Farish's runs out in May), and, as with so many labour-intensive industries, other countries are taking an ever-increasing share of the business.

41

Farish grew up in Aldershot, an army town, with a father who believed firmly in discipline. This belief engendered the opposite in his son, who, despite being bright, barely attended school and managed to leave with a bad report and an attitude problem. 'I was a bit mouthy,' he says, 'generally my own fault.'

42

He survived on what work he could find, moving on from town to town once he'd outstayed his welcome. 'At times, I loved it,' he admits, 'that total freedom from responsibility. And then it starts getting a bit cold, and you think: "Help! How am I going to eat?"'

43

Now Farish makes £30,000 a year, at least until May, and has never been happier. Despite the insecurity, the boredom, and having to explain what he does all the time, he says he loves his job – especially when the dolls get something exciting to do.

36

A Because he's known worse, these threats to his livelihood bother Farish less than most. For six years he was homeless, on and off, and even food was not guaranteed. 'I've already hit the lowest you can go,' he says.

B But even this isn't the most laborious process. That honour goes to speech, as every lip and tongue movement for every sound has to be posed and photographed, and the result must synchronise perfectly with the recorded soundtrack. The character may be pointing and simultaneously doing a little dance. Writers, on the whole, are blithely unaware of the nightmare such actions will bring for the poor wretch who translates their imaginations into reality.

C Small, stocky and shaven-headed, Farish does not immediately make one think of children's television. He works in Manchester for Cosgrove Hall, a famous old animation shop responsible for classics such as *Danger Mouse* and *Count Duckula*. The building is a warren of black baize curtains, separating a series of untidy studios. The atmosphere is one of chaos held precariously at bay.

D Towards the end of even the longest day, however, comes the moment that animators live for: pressing 'play'. 'It's a dead object,' says Farish, 'and then all of a sudden it's moving around and talking, and jumping about.' It's as if he is describing some kind of magic spell. 'You can't see until you've done it, so it's all got to be in your head until you're finished, and when you press play – that's when you find out if it all works or not.'

E Having started as a plumber's apprentice in the early 1990s, he found himself without qualifications, and then suddenly without a job when economic recession hit. 'People stopped paying each other, and I was bottom of the chain.' He was left with just a sleeping-bag, a penknife and a change of clothes to depend on.

F In fact, Farish's dedication knows no bounds. He even creates short cartoons in his spare time for his own amusement. Stop-motion is too complex and expensive to do at home, so he is teaching himself computer-generated animation. 'It started off as a bit of light relief but it's gradually taking over home life as well.'

G But then, after a period studying production management at drama school, Farish enrolled on a web-design course. One day they had an animation lesson, and out of 20 students, Farish was the only one who could do it. On his teacher's recommendation, he gave up web design and took a degree in animation. 'I never chose to be an animator,' he says. 'It never occurred to me that you could do this for a job.'

H That would not, of course, be the reaction of a child, but while a child might put a more positive spin on this, no child could muster the prodigious levels of discipline and concentration required to see the job through. All the cartoons are filmed with stop-motion animation so Farish spends his days breaking down the behaviour of his characters into thousands of tiny steps, posing the puppets into each position, and taking a picture of the scene to make a frame of film.

Test 2

Part 7

You are going to read an article about work-life balance. For questions **44–53**, choose from the sections (**A–D**). The sections may be chosen more than once. Mark your answers **on the separate answer sheet.**

Which section mentions the following?

involvement in decision-making leading to increased worker satisfaction	44
a term that was once used to refer to an inadequate work-life balance	45
a reduction in one business's expenditure caused by improved staff retention	46
a recognition among some employees of the necessity for longer working hours	47
changes in the world of work leading to competition between established and emerging companies	48
the statutory regulation of work-life balance ideas	49
certain staff benefits no longer being seen as adequate by potential employees	50
a change in how work-life balance developments are generated	51
a way of defining what work-life balance involves	52
a theory as to what people require out of life	53

38

Issues arising out of the continuing work-life debate in the UK

A

Here in the UK, the continuous pressure of work and the relentless pace of change is impacting on people. Hard. And some people have reached the point where they want their lives back or at least are questioning how they can balance their work obligations with their domestic responsibilities. This includes new recruits – employers also recognise that in the battle to attract talented people the tried and tested incentives of high salary, a medical plan and use of a company car will not pull in the high fliers any more. But what exactly does work-life balance cover? In the recent past, 'stress' was the word that best seemed to represent this general concern about too much work, too little life. Everyone understood it, since they experienced it at a personal level, but work-life balance has larger parameters. According to the Work Foundation, it is only achieved when an individual's right to a fulfilled life inside and outside paid work is respected as the norm. So, for example, work-life balance also takes into account the contribution that people want to make to the world in which they live. It includes the recognition that people have to manage family life and it considers the impact that an excessive workload has on people's health.

B

We can point to the psychologist, Abraham Maslow, as the inspiration behind the work-life balance phenomenon. Maslow's 'hierarchy of needs' model posits five ascending levels of need, each stage of which has to be satisfied in turn before the individual can move onwards and upwards. So, at the base of the triangular model, individuals first have to satisfy their physical survival needs, while at the apex of the triangle, is the 'self-actualised' individual whose priorities are personal growth and fulfilment. Maslow's work fused with a trend that also affected the concerns about work-life balance. Having a job for life, which had been part of the bedrock values of traditional companies, simply could not be sustained by the dynamic marketplace of the 1990s and beyond. The old certainties evaporated, and employers realised that the new imperative was to ensure their employees became as innovative as the young entrepreneurs who were creating exciting new businesses of their own.

C

The idea of a work-life balance has evolved over time. In the UK, there has been a long tradition of government-based initiatives that were its forerunners. However, with work-life balance as it exists today, the influence of some corporate role models has had the most impact. Consider Ben & Jerry's, the US ice-cream company. Since the 1980s, this firm has recognised that people wanted a different sort of work experience. It made a virtue out of donating 7.5 per cent of its pre-tax profits to philanthropy – an employee-led initiative. Engaging employees in such a way has helped both to improve motivation and drive innovation and productivity, making Ben & Jerry's into an extremely lucrative brand. A recent survey identified more than 100 varieties of similar work-life initiatives. However, it is clear that the most important variable in work-life balance is the nature of the job itself. People want jobs with autonomy, flexibility, meaning, managerial support as well as a chance for advancement.

D

So, do work-life balance policies work? In the UK there has been little doubt that they have had a positive impact. British Telecom, for instance, used work-life balance initiatives both to draw more women into the workforce and to address the significant problem of losing staff. As a result, a staggering 98 per cent of women returned after maternity leave, saving the organisation a tidy sum in recruitment and training. Work-life balance is already a catch-all term for many different new policy developments and the list is still growing. Many employees know from direct experience that the world of work is changing. In a 24/7 society, they recognise that their customers expect service round-the-clock. And they also know that they have to juggle their home responsibilities while stretching their schedules to meet customer expectations. Employers know this too. Indeed, there is a raft of legal provisions governing work-life balance being driven by the European Union. And what the individual employee wants and the employer is set to deliver need not be in opposition.

Test 2

WRITING (1 hour 30 minutes)

Part 1

Read the two texts below.

Write an essay summarising and evaluating the key points from both texts. Use your own words throughout as far as possible, and include your own ideas in your answers.

Write your answer in **240–280** words.

1

Movie magic

It has often been claimed that people flock to the cinema primarily to escape from the boredom, or sometimes even the misery, of their everyday lives. Remarkable technological advances have made the experience of watching a movie ever more magical and emotionally powerful, increasing the appeal and impact of the cinema for each new generation. Yet movies have a power that goes far beyond their capacity to transport us to another world, since they can influence audiences to change their attitudes or behaviour in significant ways, making them consider complex moral and social issues such as war, poverty, and prejudice.

Is the cinema in decline?

The inescapable truth is that the cinema, one of the greatest cultural achievements of the twentieth century, has reached a new low point in recent years. All but a few movies are, frankly, not worth anyone's valuable time. Audiences are increasingly presented with childish comedies, predictable action films and disappointing sequels. There is also the absurd idea that a film with an inflated budget of millions is a substitute for a well-acted, imaginative and original film. Film studios now spend almost as much money on marketing their films as producing them, which tends to suggest their concern is with profit rather than quality.

Write your **essay**.

Part 2

Write an answer to **one** of the questions **2–5** in this part. Write your answer in **280–320** words in an appropriate style.

2   You are a student at an international college. Your tutor has asked you to write an article for the college website on ways students can improve language skills outside the classroom. In your article, you should suggest ways in which students can make contact with English-language speakers. You should also assess whether the most effective way of improving language skills is to make friends with speakers of the language.

   Write your **article**.

3   An environmental organisation is inviting suggestions for new ways of raising people's awareness of the importance of protecting the countryside. You decide to write a letter in which you briefly describe your idea for a publicity campaign. You should also analyse the reasons why, in general, it is important to protect the countryside.

   Write your **letter**.

4   An English-language magazine called *Technology Today* is preparing a special edition on technological innovations of recent years such as new gadgets, applications for mobile phones or computer software. You decide to send in a review recommending something that you have found useful, briefly describing what it can do, and analysing the reasons why it has become popular.

   Write your **review**.

5   Write an answer to **one** of the following two questions based on **one** of the titles below. Write **5(a)** or **5(b)** at the beginning of your answer.

   (a)   Marc Norman and Tom Stoppard: *Shakespeare in Love*
   Your book group has asked for reports on screenplays to read in which minor characters play significant roles. You decide to write a report recommending *Shakespeare in Love* and briefly describing the roles played by three of the following: Kit (Christopher) Marlowe, the Queen, Webster and the Nurse. You should also assess any impact that these three characters had on Will or Viola.

   Write your **report**.

   (b)   Philip K Dick: *Do Androids Dream of Electric Sheep?*
   A student magazine is planning a series of articles called 'Future Visions', on some of the societies imagined by science fiction writers. You submit an article briefly describing the future world shown in *Do Androids Dream of Electric Sheep?*, and also explaining what people depend on for feelings of emotional satisfaction in this future world.

   Write your **article**.

Test 2

LISTENING (40 minutes approximately)

Part 1

You will hear three different extracts. For questions **1–6**, choose the answer (**A**, **B** or **C**) which fits best according to what you hear.

There are two questions for each extract.

Extract One

You hear a science lecturer talking to students about the sense of taste.

1 How does the lecturer feel about the so-called 'Tongue Map'?

  A surprised that it was accepted for so long
  B frustrated by the diversity of views about it
  C doubtful about whether it should continue to be used

2 Why does the lecturer refer to his own experience as a schoolchild?

  A to encourage his students to trust their own judgement
  B to show his students how scientific opinion changes over time
  C to highlight the misleading nature of some classroom experiments

Extract Two

You hear a successful businessperson, Tom Meadon, talking about his career.

3 What does Tom say benefitted him most as a young man?

  A the support of his family
  B the decision to follow his own instincts
  C the opportunities to travel to other countries

4 What is his attitude to Human Resources staff?

  A He feels they have made some unwise changes.
  B He is frustrated by their lack of commitment.
  C He wishes they would be more open-minded.

Extract Three

You hear two students, Jacky and Martin, discussing power and influence.

5 What attribute do they agree gives one person most power over another?

    A being intelligent
    B possessing great wealth
    C having an impressive job title

6 What has Jacky found out about people who are easily influenced?

    A Their status in society has little impact.
    B They frequently doubt their own abilities.
    C Their gender is a significant factor.

Test 2

Part 2

You will hear a sport psychologist called Brian Hawthorn giving a talk to psychology students about his profession.

For questions **7–15**, complete the sentences with a word or short phrase.

Brian says that sport psychologists assist both **(7)** .... and professional and amateur competitors.

Brian helps his clients deal with problems caused by **(8)** .... and emotional setbacks.

Brian says sport psychologists sometimes need to suggest ways for a trainer to improve **(9)** .... within their team.

Brian says most sport psychologists do **(10)** .... as well as private consultancy work.

According to Brian, all the techniques that sport psychologists use focus on encouraging **(11)** .... in their clients.

Brian refers to a **(12)** .... that people can make through visualisation before going to, for example, a job interview.

Brian suggests that a footballer failed because he was thinking about the **(13)** .... of his teammates.

Brian condemns the trend whereby a sportsman has **(14)** .... thrown at him from the crowd.

According to Brian, the ability to cope with **(15)** .... is what distinguishes the best sportspeople.

44

Part 3

You will hear a programme in which Rachel and Ian White talk about their office supplies company.

For questions **16–20**, choose the answer (**A, B, C** or **D**) which fits best according to what you hear.

---

16 How did the members of the Brisbane Business Network help Rachel and Ian?

    A by suggesting possible sources of funding
    B by giving them an idea of what was possible
    C by advising them against expanding too fast
    D by supporting them when they felt like giving up

17 What do Rachel and Ian say about choosing a website design company?

    A Look at other websites they have made.
    B Find out what qualifications and awards they have.
    C Check that you can contact them later if you need to.
    D Make sure they are already familiar with your type of business.

18 With regard to marketing, they recommend

    A choosing techniques that require little time.
    B checking that the database is regularly updated.
    C making frequent visits to inform clients of developments.
    D trying to build up a personal relationship with the client base.

19 When they asked for help with budgeting, they were relieved to find that

    A their business was improving.
    B they were doing better than their competitors.
    C their accounts were becoming more accurate.
    D their targets were appropriate.

20 Rachel and Ian found it useful to teach others about business plans because

    A it reminded them of things they had forgotten.
    B they got new ideas and insight from the students.
    C it helped clarify things they had not understood before.
    D they realised how much they had learned over the years.

Test 2

Part 4

You will hear five short extracts in which university students are talking about a work placement that they did.

TASK ONE

For questions **21–25**, choose from the list (**A–H**) how each speaker found their work placement.

While you listen, you must complete both tasks.

A through a family member

B on an academic website

C through a chance meeting

D on the Internet

E at a university job fair

F from a classmate's recommendation

G through a contact in the sector

H in a trade journal

Speaker 1 [ ] 21
Speaker 2 [ ] 22
Speaker 3 [ ] 23
Speaker 4 [ ] 24
Speaker 5 [ ] 25

TASK TWO

For questions **26–30**, choose from the list (**A–H**) what each speaker found most useful during the work placement.

A getting to know colleagues

B receiving feedback

C doing work-based research

D having to meet targets

E getting used to a fixed routine

F sharing opinions of proposals

G putting theories into practice

H being involved in basic procedures

Speaker 1 [ ] 26
Speaker 2 [ ] 27
Speaker 3 [ ] 28
Speaker 4 [ ] 29
Speaker 5 [ ] 30

SPEAKING (16 minutes)

There are two examiners. One (the interlocutor) conducts the test, providing you with the necessary materials and explaining what you have to do. The other examiner (the assessor) will be introduced to you, but then takes no further part in the interaction.

Part 1 (2 minutes)

The interlocutor first asks you and your partner a few questions which focus on information about yourselves.

Part 2 (4 minutes)

In this part of the test you and your partner are asked to talk together. The interlocutor places a set of pictures on the table in front of you. There may be only one picture in the set or as many as seven pictures. This stimulus provides the basis for a discussion. The interlocutor first asks an introductory question which focuses on two of the pictures (or in the case of a single picture, on aspects of the picture). After about a minute, the interlocutor gives you both a decision-making task based on the same set of pictures.

The pictures for Part 2 are on pages C4–C5 of the colour section.

Part 3 (10 minutes)

You are each given the opportunity to talk for two minutes, to comment after your partner has spoken and to take part in a more general discussion.

The interlocutor gives you a card with a question written on it and asks you to talk about it for two minutes. After you have spoken, the interlocutor asks you both another question related to the topic on the card, addressing your partner first. This procedure is repeated, so that your partner receives a card and speaks for two minutes and a follow-up question is asked.

Finally, the interlocutor asks some further questions, which leads to a discussion on a general theme related to the subjects already covered in Part 3.

The cards for Part 3 are on pages C10–C11 of the colour section.

Test 3

READING AND USE OF ENGLISH (1 hour 30 minutes)

Part 1

For questions **1–8**, read the text below and decide which answer (**A, B, C** or **D**) best fits each gap.

Mark your answers **on the separate answer sheet**.

There is an example at the beginning (**0**).

0   **A** bright   **B** polished   **C** shining   **D** glossy

0 A B **C** D

Nothing is impossible

Law firm Matthews and Reynolds is a (**0**) ..C... example of a business using art to revamp its public image. The firm hired an advertising agency called Eyeopener to carry out a rebranding (**1**) .... and gave the agency (**2**) .... rein to take the company by the scruff of the neck and effect a major makeover. The firm wanted smart, contemporary imagery which would symbolise an innovative, forward-thinking business.

(**3**) .... the firm now has a new logo, and all its advertising material features clever modern images which are (**4**) .... on the eye. Director Alan Ross comments: 'The images Eyeopener (**5**) .... say a lot about our approach, size and experience. And we were delighted with the advertising campaign they subsequently (**6**) ...., using a stylish, sophisticated approach with a touch of humour here and there.'

Public response to the rebranding has been excellent, and what appeared to be a (**7**) .... old law firm has been given a new lease of (**8**) .... as an adventurous and confident concern.

48

1 A routine   B exercise   C transaction   D function
2 A extra   B complete   C wide   D free
3 A In the end   B After all   C As a result   D In total
4 A easy   B attractive   C delightful   D agreeable
5 A stood up for   B came up with   C got through to   D fell back on
6 A portrayed   B devised   C imagined   D drafted
7 A dusty   B tedious   C murky   D monotonous
8 A fortune   B energy   C time   D life

49

Test 3

Part 2

For questions **9–16**, read the text below and think of the word which best fits each space. Use only **one** word in each space. There is an example at the beginning (**0**). Write your answers **IN CAPITAL LETTERS on the separate answer sheet**

Example: | 0 | T | O |

Neologisms – creating new words

To survive, language must evolve, yet it is resistant (**0**) ...TO.... certain forms of change. Most new words sparkle briefly, (**9**) .... at all, and then fade away. However, new words are necessary because, as the world changes, (**10**) .... must our vocabulary. In a society (**11**) .... science seems to occupy the intellectual high ground, it is inevitable that vocabularies are continually being augmented (**12**) .... technical terms.

Novel items of vocabulary distress people for two reasons. They attest to phenomena we don't like (**13**) .... expect not to like, and their tone offends our sensibilities. There is (**14**) .... new about this aversion to neologism. As far (**15**) .... as the 1750s, a distinguished English lexicographer criticised the 'unnecessary words creeping into the language'.

So what does make a word stick? First of all, it has to be widely adopted; it also has to denote something of lasting significance for it will only last as long as the phenomenon (**16**) .... question; and to become embedded, it needs to generate derivative forms.

Part 3

For questions **17–24**, read the text below. Use the word given in capitals at the end of some of the lines to form a word that fits in the space in the same line. There is an example at the beginning (**0**). Write your answers **IN CAPITAL LETTERS on the separate answer sheet**.

Example: `0 I N I T I A T I V E S`

Looking ahead to 2050

There are no guarantees as to what life will be like midway through the
21st century, but there are scientific **(0)** ..INITIATIVES.. which offer an interesting   **INITIATE**
glimpse into the future. Many people will work from home, electric cars will
be the typical form of transport, and goods and services paid for by mobile
phone. The most advanced smart homes will be **(17)** ....   **ENVIRONS**
friendly, equipped with their own **(18)** .... units which will be able   **CYCLE**
to make **(19)** .... waste water completely safe and palatable.   **DRINK**

Advances in medical science will also have far-reaching **(20)** .... ; people   **SEQUENCE**
born today can have a life **(21)** .... of 100 years. The development of   **EXPECT**
so-called smart medicine research suggests that people will carry out their
own digital health checks, enabling online analysts to reach an immediate
(22) .... of any condition requiring treatment.   **DIAGNOSE**

Scientists predict with reasonable **(23)** .... that some of these   **CERTAIN**
technological advances will be in place for many people worldwide, whereas the
nature of other changes remains **(24)** .... for the time being.   **SPECULATE**

Part 4

For questions **25–30**, complete the second sentence so that it has a similar meaning to the first sentence, using the word given **Do not change the word given**. You must use between **three** and **eight** words, including the word given. Here is an example (**0**).

Example:

0 Do you mind if I watch you while you paint?

   objection

   Do you .... you while you paint?

| 0 | have any objection to my watching |

Write **only** the missing words **on the separate answer sheet**.

---

25 Don't let Sarah's carefree attitude deceive you; she's an extremely conscientious worker.

   taken

   Don't let .... Sarah's carefree attitude; she's an extremely conscientious worker.

26 Fred didn't tell Sophie his news until she had finished her homework.

   for

   Fred .... telling her his news.

27 Although I am angry about what happened, in no circumstances would I want anyone to intervene on my behalf.

   last

   Although I am angry about what happened, the .... anyone to intervene on my behalf.

28 There is a rumour that the company lost over $20 million during the price war.

sustained

The company is rumoured ……………………………………………… over $20 million during the price war.

29 I ought to have had the roof repaired in the summer rather than leaving it until the autumn.

better

It ……………………………………… had the roof repaired in the summer rather than leaving it until the autumn.

30 Alex made regular calls to his parents while travelling abroad.

kept

Alex ……………………………………… his parents by phone while travelling abroad.

Part 5

You are going to read a newspaper article about libraries. For questions **31–36**, choose the answer (**A**, **B**, **C** or **D**) which you think fits best according to the text. Mark your answers **on the separate answer sheet**.

Why libraries matter in today's technological world

Municipal libraries are perhaps one of the most enduring public institutions – priceless repositories of history, language, and culture. The dawn of the 'information superhighway' threatened to make them less relevant, even obsolete. Yet now, these institutions are extending their mission well beyond the storage of knowledge. Indeed, to distinguish themselves in a world where Google is well on its way to digitally scanning most of the books ever written, libraries are learning to avail themselves of the simple fact that they are centrally located in almost every community in the USA. In other words, libraries now see success being linked to their role as public places and destinations.

While many US cities and towns now recognize the importance of re-inventing public libraries as destinations, this awareness doesn't always translate into a well-rounded success. The most high-profile new libraries rely on stylized designs to create buzz, feeding a false perception that public libraries are all about attention-grabbing looks. But when the tour bus crowds stop coming, these libraries will sink or swim based on how well they serve the needs of their respective communities – whether they are truly great places, not just eye-catching buildings.

There are plenty of unsung libraries that embody a very different and more compelling vision of what it means to be a public place. They may fly under the radar as architectural landmarks, but they still garner respect, praise and even adoration on account of their innovative management and programming. They are taking on a larger civic role – balancing their traditional needs and operations with outreach to the wider community – thereby contributing to the creation of a physical commons that benefits the public as a whole. If the traditional model of the library was the inward-focused community 'reading room', the current one is more like a community 'front porch'. *line 14* *line 15* *line 19* *line 20*

But what of universities and other academic institutions; what is the value of an academic library in an age of abundant information? A recent report commissioned by the Online Computer Library Center focusing on college students found that they use libraries more than any other demographic group, that they like to help themselves to information, that they are aware of the library's electronic resources, and that they identify libraries with books (but they don't seem to feel that's a bad thing, unlike the so called experts who authored the report who reveal deep dismay at that finding). What's more, they supplement library resources with ones found on the web (no surprise there; don't we all?), they are largely satisfied with services and facilities and they are strongly attached to the idea of libraries.

For college students, the library is like the poet Robert Frost's idea of home, 'the place where, when you have to go there, they have to take you in.' They may not want to be there, they may not have any real curiosity about the topic they are researching, but the library is a gateway to the sources they need, and for at least some students the librarians are 'saviors' who help them take an assignment and locate sources that will match.

Of course, these days any distinction between library and digital information is obsolete. But there is a valid distinction between printed book and the web, as there is between library and home computer. And the fact is, there are things that the web cannot offer which any library can. In a library it's the totality of the experience that matters: the website, the face-to-face services, the catalog, the collection. Staff are on hand to ensure the user's reaction to the library is positive and productive, especially the novice user. Moreover, a library creates relationships. It develops in users a sense of belonging, both to the library community, whether local or academic, and to the wider world of knowledge. In this and other respects, the billions of web pages in existence do not carry the same symbolic weight as the library. It stands for the importance of knowledge, for access, for the idea that pursuing questions is a valuable human endeavor. We would do well not to dismiss that symbolism as mere nostalgia.

Reading and Use of English

31 What point is the writer making about public libraries in the first paragraph?

    A They are struggling to survive in the digital age.
    B They will have to find a completely new purpose.
    C They are taking full advantage of an existing benefit.
    D They may well have to give up their function of storing books.

32 In the second paragraph, the writer's purpose is to

    A warn libraries against trusting in new buildings to attract users.
    B praise libraries which recognize the benefits of tourism.
    C stress the need for libraries to consult local residents.
    D advise libraries to move to more central locations.

33 Which phrase illustrates 'a very different and more compelling vision of what it means to be a public place'? (lines 14–15)

    A they may fly under the radar (line 15)
    B architectural landmarks (line 15)
    C community 'reading room' (line 19)
    D community 'front porch' (line 20)

34 What is the writer emphasising in the first bracketed comment in the fourth paragraph?

    A her contempt for the reaction of the report writers
    B her concern for the outdated attitudes of the students
    C her doubt about the range of library users that were questioned
    D her distrust regarding the motives of those commissioning the report

35 Why does the writer quote the poet Robert Frost's definition of home?

    A to underline the literary value of a library's resources
    B to describe the function an academic library is required to fulfil
    C to suggest the paternal role taken by some college librarians
    D to express the sense of comfort libraries used to give their readers

36 In comparing libraries and the Internet, the writer

    A is urging libraries to concentrate on doing what they do best.
    B suggests there is no essential difference between them.
    C is making the case for the existence of libraries as a separate entity.
    D appears to regard libraries as an unnecessary luxury.

Test 3

Part 6

You are going to read a magazine article about white-water rafting. Seven paragraphs have been removed from the extract. Choose from the paragraphs **A–H** the one which fits each gap (**37–43**). There is one extra paragraph which you do not need to use. Mark your answers **on the separate answer sheet**.

A Wet and Wonderful Ride

Cameron Wilson is swept away by the thrill of Tasmania's formidable Franklin River

Tasmania's Franklin River is a renowned rafting destination, both for the beauty and remoteness of the country through which it flows and for the challenge it presents the rafter. I'd been told by one of the guides on my trip that 'portage' is an indispensable word in the river rafter's lexicon. It derives from the French where it means 'physically carrying boats between two navigable stretches of a river'.

| 37 |

Such is the challenge of expedition rafting and the truth is, I was loving every minute of it. I glanced over at Brendan, at twenty-one the younger of our two river guides, and his grin confirmed that he too was having a ball, despite appearing in imminent danger of being swept off his feet and into the torrent. 'Mate,' he yelled over the roar of the rapids, 'like I keep telling them... this is not a holiday!'

| 38 |

A measure of respect, therefore, seemed in order, as I psyched myself up for rafting through the heart of the wilderness that had been so hard fought for. I was one of a group of ten – eight clients plus two guides – mustered over an early breakfast in Collingwood Bridge, two and a half hours north-west of the Tasmanian capital, Hobart.

| 39 |

A light drizzle was beginning to close in as we donned helmets and life-jackets, and pushed off into the gentle currents of a calm tributary. It was plain sailing so far, but I knew these tranquil waters would carry us on down to the raging Franklin. The afternoon was spent becoming acquainted with our raft buddies, or with pressing Shaun and Brendan for stories about Franklin expeditions from days gone by.

| 40 |

Thanks to the light but steady rain, however, the river level turned out to be high enough for us to glide over small rocks, and portage comfortably around the bigger ones, on the way to our first campsite. Conditions there turned out to be typical of those for the entire trip; the ravine drops steeply to the river and there is not much level ground, so rock overhangs make handy shelters.

| 41 |

The summit is more than half a vertical mile above the Franklin. It's the perfect spot from which to take in the unspoilt beauty of the country we'd been travelling through, its mountains, forests, high-country lakes and tarns.

| 42 |

Ironically enough, it was not until we struck one of the less celebrated stretches of white water that our only real rafting drama occurred. Shaun and his crew had wrapped their raft around a boulder and there it stayed for twenty minutes, held in place by the fast-flowing white water.

| 43 |

As the river widened, such white-knuckle experiences became fewer and further between, and as we eased into a leisurely paddling rhythm, twice I caught sight of platypus crossing the river. The silences grew longer and more comfortable, and as we slipped along under a blue sky the quiet was broken now and then by Shaun enquiring: 'How's the serenity?' On each occasion it was well above par.

56

A Having hung gamely on for a minute or two, Simon, a tax auditor from Brisbane, was finally dragged away for a bumpy solo ride to the bottom of the cascades. He came up bruised but smiling. I think it summed up how we were all feeling about the trip at that point.

B I had reason to reflect upon this information as I scrambled about on a slippery rock, trying to carry a heavy rubber raft between two boulders. The gap was too narrow and I was under constant assault from thousands of litres of white water. However expressed, this was a skill you couldn't do without if you were going to raft down the Franklin.

C It just went to prove how right our guide had been. A Franklin expedition is not a joy ride. It is, however, an opportunity to experience life on a river that, thanks to those who campaigned to save it, survives as one of the world's great wilderness journeys.

D Some of the stretches we'd be doing could be rafted straight through apparently, with the boulders under two metres of water. At other times the river gets so low we'd have to do a high portage – unload the gear, deflate and carry the lot through the forest. But you never knew because the river presents a new challenge each and every time.

E The moment arrived to pack our gear and supplies into barrels and 'dry bags' and lash these to aluminium frames, which were then secured in the two rafts. Our trip leader, Shaun, briefed us on how to handle a difficult portage or riding a rugged set of rapids, and talked us through ways of getting back into a raft from which you've just tumbled.

F The next few days saw both raft crews functioning superbly as we traversed the next section of river, responding as one to commands, as we bounced off logs and boulders through rapids. These were evocatively referred to by names such as 'The Cauldron', 'Nasty Notch' and 'Thunderush'.

G There was no doubting the truth of this assertion. I'd chosen this trip for a number of reasons, not least the fact that the Franklin is famous for the events of 1983. That's when thousands of people took to the streets or chained themselves to bulldozers to save it from being dammed and flooded, in what remains one of the largest environmental campaigns in Australia's history.

H Roused by Brendan, we'd be coaxed from our cocoons each day with the aroma of fresh coffee. On the day of our third such awakening, the sky had cleared beautifully, which meant fleece jackets and waterproofs could give way to dark glasses and sunscreen. The conditions were ideal for the long day's hike to Frenchman's Cap.

Test 3

Part 7

You are going to read an article about ballet. For questions **44–53**, choose from the sections (**A–D**). The sections may be chosen more than once. Mark your answers **on the separate answer sheet**.

In which section does the writer mention

the level of fitness needed to engage in an activity?	44
an explanation of the remedial health benefits of an activity?	45
being surprised to see an outcome in a short space of time?	46
ballet exercises as a form of escapism?	47
a feeling of contentment arising out of physical activity?	48
chance remarks that were a source of inspiration?	49
the challenging range of skills and abilities required by ballet?	50
the idea that people should attempt something beyond their normal capabilities?	51
how an activity might be unfairly regarded by some people?	52
the effect of the activity on the ability to resist an indulgence?	53

58

Is ballet the new gym?

Celebrities are not alone in finding ballet training gives them a good workout, says Abigail Hoffman

A

I always find the winter months difficult here in London, but exercise can help to beat the winter blues because during any exercise routine, the body produces 'happy' endorphins. With attractive flushed cheeks and a warm glow of post-exercise smugness, you will feel much better than if you were suffering the inevitable side-effects of other types of weight-loss programme. I'm not suggesting you high-tail it to the gym, however. Gyms are anathema to many, who perceive them as overly competitive and so twentieth century. No, I'm recommending that you follow the example of celebrities and take to the barre. Devotees in New York, London and Paris cite suppleness, strength and a sculpted silhouette as the chief benefits of a ballet-based fitness regime. Deride it, if you will, as the latest media-fuelled fad, but increasingly exercise professionals are referring to ballet as the 'new Pilates'. Its benefits have also been noted by the New Zealand rugby team, who have been known to incorporate ballet moves into their training routine.

B

Charlotte Toner, a former professional ballerina, has been at the forefront of this trend. Some years ago, she developed what is known as her 'floor barre' class, which incorporates elementary ballet and Pilates-type movements. 'I fell into teaching it because my friends were always asking how I kept in shape,' she says. 'Then I discovered there was so much demand that I had to get my act together and produce a proper timetable.' Injured dancers often do floor barre because as the name implies, you work mainly lying on the floor rather than standing at the barre. Since the back is supported, it's relatively risk-free. Joy Waiter, a leading physiotherapist, says: 'This combination of movement and stretch, underpinned by stability, is a good model for most people with back problems. Floor barre is also an ideal exercise routine for those not in the first flush of youth.' Ballet's focus on lengthening rather than contracting muscles promotes flexibility, maintaining a lithe appearance. 'If you attend class regularly, you'll be noticing a difference in body shape in no time,' Charlotte assured me.

C

Charlotte offers a variety of classes, each lasting seventy-five minutes, and can accommodate complete beginners at floor barre as well as advanced ballet performers. Participants span the generations and it's comforting to realise that you don't need the co-ordination skills of an acrobat or the stamina of an Olympic marathon runner to attempt a plié at the barre. 'If you can walk on a treadmill,' she insists, 'you can do floor barre.' Co-ordination, elegance and suppleness come with practice. I was recommended to take up floor barre when persistent lower back pain prevented me from working out in the gym. After a mere six-week course with Charlotte, attending three sessions a week, my back improved and muscle tone was starting to replace dimpled flab. I also lost 4.5kg effortlessly; somehow glimpsing my podgy reflection in triplicate in the studio mirrors eviscerated my desire for chips and chocolate.

D

But the appeal goes beyond the visible results; many devotees highlight another side of ballet. 'It's about expressing myself in a different way,' one says. 'The melodic music transports you far from the daily grind.' Françoise Peretti, managing director of her own public-relations firm, puts it well. 'Ballet tones my body but it also tones my soul,' she says. 'As a former investment banker used to analysing the nuances of financial markets, I was unprepared for how ballet challenges the intellect as well as the body. There's a litany of things to remember and it calls for both concentration and mental agility. Co-ordinating your arms and legs is difficult enough but you also have to simultaneously stand tall, lower your shoulders, breathe correctly and memorise the often complex routines.' So, if you too are gazing despondently at the overcast sky, wondering desperately how you're ever going to get through the winter months as you long to burrow back under the bedcovers, think about shaking a leg – literally. Step outside your comfort zone and treat yourself to a fitness regime that is fun, uplifting and very effective. Take up floor barre. Your thighs will thank you for it.

Test 3

WRITING (1 hours 30 minutes)

Part 1

Read the two texts below.

Write an essay summarising and evaluating the key points from both texts. Use your own words throughout as far as possible, and include your own ideas in your answers.

Write your answer in **240–280** words.

1

Eating together

It is often said that a pleasure shared is a pleasure doubled, and who can deny that conversation around the dinner table provides opportunities for a family or friends to share their happiness, express their feelings and learn from one another. Meals taken together foster warmth, security and love, as well as feelings of belonging. This unifying role that food can play in our lives can be seen on a much bigger scale, too. Many cultures have rich culinary traditions, and the distinctiveness or the quality of their food can be a powerful source of pride, strengthening a sense of cultural or national identity.

Food, glorious food!

In today's undeniably stressful, fast-moving world, the increasing popularity of convenience food should come as no surprise. Despite warnings from doctors about the possible health risks of such food, it is all too easy to pop something in the microwave every day, and in so doing miss out on one of life's great experiences, which is cooking fresh food. Not only does preparing home-made food give satisfaction, and the results taste immeasurably better than the tinned or packaged variety, but, more significantly, it gives the opportunity to display care and affection through hospitality shown to guests.

Write your **essay**.

Part 2

Write an answer to **one** of the questions **2–5** in this part. Write your answer in **280–320** words in an appropriate style.

2   Your college magazine has asked its readers to send in reviews of the leisure opportunities available in the nearby town. You decide to submit a review of a sports centre in town. In your review you should briefly describe the facilities available, and assess the extent to which you consider that it meets the needs of the students.

   Write your **review**.

3   An international magazine is planning a feature on the importance of understanding the past. You decide to write a letter in which you briefly describe an important event in your country's history which you think everybody ought to be aware of. You should also explain the extent to which we can ever understand the present without knowing about the past.

   Write your **letter**.

4   An English-language newspaper is inviting readers to contribute to a series of articles about interesting possessions that have been handed down to them by family members. You decide to write an article about something you have inherited from a family member. You should describe what it is and explain why, in general, you think it is important to pass on interesting possessions to future generations.

   Write your **article**.

5   Write an answer to **one** of the following two questions based on **one** of the titles below. Write **5(a)** or **5(b)** at the beginning of your answer.

   (a)   Marc Norman and Tom Stoppard: *Shakespeare in Love*
         An English-language newspaper has invited readers to send in reviews of screenplays based on the theme of mistaken identities and the misunderstandings that result. You decide to submit a review of *Shakespeare In Love*. Your review should briefly describe how different characters mislead one another, explain why they do so and consider whether their behaviour has any serious consequences.

         Write your **review**.

   (b)   Philip K Dick: *Do Androids Dream of Electric Sheep?*
         You have been studying *Do Androids Dream of Electric Sheep?* in your English language lessons, and your tutor has asked you to write an essay on bounty hunters. In your essay, you should briefly describe the characters of Rick Deckard and Phil Resch and the work they do, and assess the extent to which you think their attitudes to their job change in the course of the novel.

         Write your **essay**.

Test 3

LISTENING (40 minutes approximately)

Part 1

You will hear three different extracts.

For questions **1–6**, choose the answer (**A**, **B** or **C**) which fits best according to what you hear.

There are two questions for each extract.

Extract One

You hear an art gallery guide talking about the paintings of Marianne North, a nineteenth-century traveller and botanical artist.

1 The guide suggests that Marianne North's work is important

   A as historical documentation.
   B for its range of subject matter.
   C because of technical expertise.

2 The guide refers to a change in people's attitude towards

   A the role of education.
   B the value of artistic skills.
   C the relationships between men and women.

Extract Two

You hear part of an interview with Professor Renton, who has recently been appointed director of a science museum.

3 What does Professor Renton suggest that he has inherited?

   A his enquiring mind
   B his problem-solving skills
   C his talent for gathering facts

4 Professor Renton says that one of the museum's aims should be to

   A reassure visitors about current issues.
   B enable visitors to draw conclusions.
   C interpret evidence for visitors.

Listening

Extract Three

You hear an economist talking about technological developments.

5 What is his attitude towards the Internet?

    A Its practical drawbacks have been overemphasised.
    B Its effects on business have generally been exaggerated.
    C Its social importance has been overestimated by entrepreneurs.

6 What does he say about washing machines?

    A They led to an expansion of the labour market.
    B They were initially only available to wealthier people.
    C They were an early sign of changing attitudes to women.

Test 3

Part 2

You will hear part of a lecture about ancient Egyptian ships and an attempt to reconstruct one. For questions **7–15**, complete the sentences with a word or short phrase.

Archaeologists believe that the site called Mersa Gawasis was once a (7) .... on the Red Sea.

To gain the support from the (8) ...., the Pharaoh Hatshepsut imported incense by ship.

Ancient Egyptian shipbuilders differed from modern ones in that they did not make a (9) .... for the ship they were building.

The speaker compares building an ancient Egyptian ship to doing a (10) ....

The Egyptian river ship used (11) .... to help attach planks together, unlike the seagoing ships.

Wood from trees grown in (12) .... was used in the reconstruction of the ship.

The modern shipbuilders were provided with a (13) .... by the archaeologists.

The modern shipbuilders used (14) .... to make the ship watertight.

The modern team used a (15) .... to get the ship to the sea.

Part 3

You will hear two costume design students, Angela and Mike, discussing the role of costumes in films.

For questions **16–20**, choose the answer (**A**, **B**, **C** or **D**) which fits best according to what you hear.

---

16   At the beginning of their course, they were asked to watch a film with the sound turned off to see if they could

   A   still follow the details of the plot.
   B   spot small inconsistencies in costumes.
   C   identify the main themes of the film.
   D   predict the development of characters' relationships.

17   Which aspect of the course particularly interests Mike?

   A   the importance of film as social history
   B   the way film influences fashion
   C   costume-making techniques
   D   the sourcing of fashion accessories

18   What interpretation of a female character wearing layers of clothes do they find implausible?

   A   that she is shy and lacks confidence
   B   that she has a complex personality
   C   that she wants to hide her past
   D   that she is still searching for her true identity

19   What compromise do they agree costume designers have to make?

   A   They have to sacrifice authenticity for dramatic effect.
   B   They have to make costumes that are comfortable for actors to wear.
   C   They substitute poorer-quality fabrics because of budget constraints.
   D   They carry out limited research because of tight deadlines.

20   What is Angela going to do her next project on?

   A   how to make costumes for films with large numbers of minor characters
   B   how to alter costumes to reflect the development of the main character
   C   how the significance of items of clothing has changed over time
   D   how male film-makers have misunderstood the role of women

Part 4

You will hear five short extracts in which people are talking about their experiences in their first jobs.

TASK ONE

For questions **21–25**, choose from the list (**A–H**) what skill each speaker developed during their first job.

TASK TWO

For questions **26–30**, choose from the list (**A–H**) what each speaker appreciated most in their first job.

While you listen, you must complete both tasks.

TASK ONE

A translating
B time management
C giving presentations
D financial planning
E giving feedback
F interpreting data
G problem solving
H delegating tasks

Speaker 1 [ ] 21
Speaker 2 [ ] 22
Speaker 3 [ ] 23
Speaker 4 [ ] 24
Speaker 5 [ ] 25

TASK TWO

A the friendliness of colleagues
B flexible working hours
C out-of-work activities
D hands-on learning style
E the opportunity to deal with a challenge
F travel opportunities
G financial incentives
H promotion opportunity

Speaker 1 [ ] 26
Speaker 2 [ ] 27
Speaker 3 [ ] 28
Speaker 4 [ ] 29
Speaker 5 [ ] 30

SPEAKING (16 minutes)

There are two examiners. One (the interlocutor) conducts the test, providing you with the necessary materials and explaining what you have to do. The other examiner (the assessor) will be introduced to you, but then takes no further part in the interaction.

Part 1 (2 minutes)

The interlocutor first asks you and your partner a few questions which focus on information about yourselves.

Part 2 (4 minutes)

In this part of the test you and your partner are asked to talk together. The interlocutor places a set of pictures on the table in front of you. There may be only one picture in the set or as many as seven pictures. This stimulus provides the basis for a discussion. The interlocutor first asks an introductory question which focuses on two of the pictures (or in the case of a single picture, on aspects of the picture). After about a minute, the interlocutor gives you both a decision-making task based on the same set of pictures.

The pictures for Part 2 are on pages C6–C7 of the colour section.

Part 3 (10 minutes)

You are each given the opportunity to talk for two minutes, to comment after your partner has spoken and to take part in a more general discussion.

The interlocutor gives you a card with a question written on it and asks you to talk about it for two minutes. After you have spoken, the interlocutor asks you both another question related to the topic on the card, addressing your partner first. This procedure is repeated, so that your partner receives a card and speaks for two minutes and a follow-up question is asked.

Finally, the interlocutor asks some further questions, which leads to a discussion on a general theme related to the subjects already covered in Part 3.

The cards for Part 3 are on pages C10–C11 of the colour section.

Test 4

READING AND USE OF ENGLISH (1 hour 30 minutes)

Part 1

For questions **1–8**, read the text below and decide which answer (**A**, **B**, **C** or **D**) best fits each gap.

Mark your answers **on the separate answer sheet**.

There is an example at the beginning (**0**).

| 0 | A | managed | B | functioned | C | performed | D | worked |

0 A B C **D**

Photography at its most daring

Photographers who have **(0)** ....D.... so close to volcanoes that their clothes started to burn, come within stroking **(1)** .... of tigers in the wild, or dived under sea ice in freezing cold water have **(2)** .... forces for an exhibition, **(3)** .... as displaying images from the harshest places on Earth

Polar bears and seals were **(4)** .... on camera by a photographer who grew up in the Arctic and trained as a **(5)** .... biologist. He dives under sea ice to swim with his subjects, once offending a leopard seal by **(6)** .... the penguin she tried to feed him with. Another exhibitor has recorded not only tigers but also chimpanzees that had never before encountered human beings. The volcano enthusiasts work in fireproof suits, always at risk of becoming so **(7)** .... by the beauty of the eruptions that they venture too close. There are invisible pockets of gas as well as flames, all of which contribute to the **(8)** .... perils of being an extreme photographer.

68

1	A interval	B space	C distance	D reach
2	A united	B joined	C merged	D integrated
3	A billed	B announced	C labelled	D scheduled
4	A snatched	B captured	C taken	D suspended
5	A aquatic	B sea	C marine	D ocean
6	A repulsing	B denying	C dismissing	D refusing
7	A transfixed	B bound	C focussed	D held
8	A reckless	B deadly	C alarming	D fearful

Part 2

For questions **9–16**, read the text below and think of the word which best fits each space. Use only one word in each space. There is an example at the beginning (**0**). Write your answers **IN CAPITAL LETTERS on the separate answer sheet**.

Example: **0** A M O U N T

Altering the modern mind

A recently published book claims that the (**0**) AMOUNT of time we spend on the Internet is changing the very structure of our brains. Its thesis is simple enough: not only that the modern world's relentless informational overload is killing our capacity (**9**) .... reflection, contemplation and patience, but that our online habits are also altering the way our brains are wired.

In the book, the author looks (**10**) .... on such human inventions as the map and the clock and the (**11**) .... to which they influenced our essential models of thought. He argues that the Internet's multiplicity of stimuli and mass of information have (**12**) .... rise to hurried and distracted thinking. Without putting too fine a point on it, the author concludes that our ability to learn (**13**) .... at all worthwhile has become superficial. Surprisingly very (**14**) .... research has looked into the Internet's effects on the brain, but further research is (**15**) .... hand and is investigating whether deep-thinking processes really are in (**16**) .... of disappearing.

Part 3

For questions **17–24**, read the text below. Use the word given in capitals at the end of some of the lines to form a word that fits in the space in the same line. There is an example at the beginning (**0**). Write your answers **IN CAPITAL LETTERS on the separate answer sheet**.

Example: `0 G L O B A L`

Windfarms

Windfarms are hailed as powerful weapons in the battle against (**0**) ..GLOBAL.. warming; it is considered by many to be politically incorrect to criticise them. They are clean, green and therefore (**17**) ……………, and viewed as such throughout the world. There is a (**18**) …………… to wind turbines, of course. They are enormous and dominate the landscape; they make a noise that condemns people to (**19**) …………… nights. One turbine standing alone in a windswept setting could be described as beautiful, but can the same description be applied to a whole host of them? But all these drawbacks pale into (**20**) ……………, we are told, compared to the great benefits that will result from this renewable energy source.

GLOBE

VIRTUE

SIDE

SLEEP

SIGNIFY

However, there is as yet no economic way of storing electricity; turbines generate it only when the wind blows, not (**21**) …………… when demand is high; (**22**) …………… of carbon from the plants manufacturing turbines are considerable. (**23**) ……………, the environmental pollution caused by the extraction of a metal crucial to their construction is potentially (**24**) …………… .

NECESSARY
EMIT
ADD
DISASTER

71

Test 4

Part 4

For questions **25–30**, complete the second sentence so that it has a similar meaning to the first sentence, using the word given. **Do not change the word given.** You must use between **three** and **eight** words, including the word given. Here is an example (**0**).

Example:

0 Do you mind if I watch you while you paint?

objection

Do you .... you while you paint?

| **0** | have any objection to my watching |

Write **only** the missing words **on the separate answer sheet**.

---

25 Unless Sam's plans change over the weekend, we'll leave early on Monday morning.

no

Providing .... over the weekend, we'll leave early on Monday morning.

26 As far as I know, Simon will be here on Thursday.

suppose

I've .... be here on Thursday.

27 The role played by the PR company in securing the government contract was never acknowledged officially.

official

At no time .... the role the PR company played securing the government contract.

72

28 Passengers are absolutely forbidden to cross the railway track.

account

On ………………………………………… to cross the railway track.

29 I have no idea why my email bounced back.

loss

I ………………………………………… why my email bounced back.

30 Felix doesn't intend to make the same mistake again.

no

Felix ………………………………………… the same mistake again.

Part 5

You are going to read a newspaper article about people's attitudes to their possessions in a digital age. For questions **31–36**, choose the answer (**A**, **B**, **C** or **D**) which you think fits best according to the text. Mark your answers **on the separate answer sheet**.

Less is More

How do people cut down on their possessions in a digital age

The 17th century French artist Poussin is well-known for his paintings, usually set in serene and idyllic pastoral landscapes, which convey serious lessons for mankind. These messages are sometimes a bit obscure, and some continue to puzzle art historians, but in the picture *Landscape with Diogenes*, things seem relatively straightforward. The ancient philosopher Diogenes is depicted casting away his last possession, a drinking bowl. He realises he doesn't need it after seeing a youth cupping a hand to drink from a river. The significance for us is that Diogenes' spiritual descendants known as 'new minimalists' are now everywhere, if not as radically possession-free as he was.

There are hundreds of websites extolling the virtues of uncluttered living. 'I can carry everything I own,' says Kevin. 'I have a few changes of clothing, laptop, two pots, bowl, spoon, fork, futon and flask. I like sitting on the floor eating fruit, nuts, vegetables and rice.' At this point I really hated Kevin, but I should have known better because he continued, 'The nice thing about a bare room is that you begin to notice other things like the changing sunlight during the day. Many possessions tend to tie one down mentally and physically – seeing too much permanence in inanimate objects rather than being aware of the vitality of the outside world of nature.'

Everyone is trying to cut down on things these days. People are trying to reduce their carbon footprints, their waistlines, their monthly outgoings. What's more, there's a general fear that people are becoming asphyxiated by their possessions, and this is fuelled by the knowledge that, according to innumerable sociological surveys, the leading pastime these days seems to be shopping. It's true, sales of e-readers and e-books outstrip those of paperbacks, and we know that only losers and reactionaries buy camera film today. As a result, the need for bookshelves and photo albums is cut out.

However, today's new minimalists don't urge us to burn our books and crush our CDs, but just make sure we have them as digital files. So, for example, I have digitised versions of some of my old vinyl LP records and haven't, as yet, stirred myself to take the LPs to the nearest charity shop – and I admit I shall probably go on keeping them. Technology has, perhaps, gone beyond our dreams and there is always the lurking suspicion that our hard drives will crash and all will be lost. Far more important, however, is the fact that our memories are so inextricably tied to our possessions that we can't get rid of stuff. No matter how much glossy magazines insist that we should.

We are not exactly suffering withdrawal symptoms as we try to break our addiction to objects. We are just acquiring new stuff that means we can bin or recycle our old stuff. Diogenes, who was quite the cynic philosopher, would have seen through this imposture in seconds. Those who can afford to, buy the kit to make the minimalist dream a reality, but they are still investing in commodities, just different ones from those they collected a decade earlier.

A few years ago I wrote a piece predicting the demise of incredibly expensive watches, believing that they would inevitably be eclipsed by the amazingly more versatile mobile phone, no matter how beautifully crafted and elegant they might be, but they still seem to be covetable objects of conspicuous consumption. Clearly the ostensible function of a £20k watch is negligible enticement to owning it. Here then is another manifestation of the lure of possessions – we are not only sentimental in our attachment to them, but also status driven.

I'm happy to have found another website which seems to solve a whole lot of problems at once – a thriving online advice surgery offering storage solutions. The interior designer responsible for this does not counsel getting rid of stuff, but rather recommends buying more stuff (elegant flexible trugs, colourful lidded containers) to hide the first lot of stuff from view. I love this philosophy – get that decluttered minimalist look, convince yourself you've got your desire for possessions under control, without having to lose a thing. There's no reason to think such bad faith will change soon: we aren't ruthless enough to emulate Diogenes and cast away all our possessions.

31 Why does the writer refer to a painting by the artist Poussin?

    A Its message is not as simple as it appears.

    B Its meaning is only now becoming clear.

    C It illustrates a very modern trend.

    D It portrays a very wise philosopher.

32 What lesson did the writer take from his own reaction to Kevin's blog?

    A Learn to enjoy your natural surroundings.

    B Don't be too quick to judge people.

    C Take pleasure in the simple things of life.

    D Don't become tied down by possessions.

33 In the writer's opinion, what prompts people to want to reduce their possessions?

    A unease about the acquisitive nature of modern society

    B a desire to take advantage of new technology

    C a concern about wasting money

    D an urge to simplify their lives

34 The writer thinks minimalism will not succeed in the long term because of people's

    A lack of faith in digital hardware.

    B laziness in the face of change.

    C nostalgia for physical objects.

    D resistance to media pressure.

35 The writer suggests Diogenes would have viewed modern attempts at minimalism with

    A indifference.

    B sympathy.

    C approval.

    D contempt.

36 According to the writer, people invest in smart new storage in order to

    A ease their conscience over having too many things.

    B provide a temporary solution to a problem.

    C make attractive additions to their homes.

    D indulge their desire to make purchases.

Part 6

You are going to read a newspaper article about psychology. Seven paragraphs have been removed from the extract. Choose from the paragraphs **A–H** the one which fits each gap (**37–43**). There is one extra paragraph which you do not need to use. Mark your answers **on the separate answer sheet**.

Psychology: just common sense?

For many sceptics, it was a sweet moment when, at a recent science meeting, a psychology professor denounced his own discipline as 'banal' and 'a fake science'. As a rehearsal for an international conference on the theme of 'critical psychology', Professor Ian Parker was addressing the British Psychology Association.

37

So it was a relief for some to hear of Professor Parker's claim that psychologists 'don't tell us anything we don't already know'. The rebel professor argues that psychology cannot claim to be a science because it is unable to subject itself to the same research and validation processes that biology, physics and chemistry do. This accusation has been made loudly for decades and he says the subject has done little to improve itself. 'Psychology pretends to be a science but it is not a science and it is questionable whether it could ever be one,' he says.

38

For a long time, psychologists have attempted to address the issue of what effect this attitude has. Some have incorporated into their conclusions the influence it has on results, exposing it instead of making ineffectual attempts to hide it. And new, more sophisticated theories have arisen. Professor Parker thinks a few of these have been useful but most are merely fads: 'They are there for about 10 years and then they disappear.'

39

Professor Parker accepts that these may be cheap experiment fodder. But, he argues, how many of us feel that their behaviour yields much insight into the rest of us? In some institutions, he claims, it is now becoming compulsory for them to take part in psychology experiments, narrowing even further the range of people that is studied.

40

Thus, the psychologist who studies, say, impulse buying, must first test our preconceptions about the habit to decide on common views on it. After that, he then makes more detailed investigations to see if the evidence supports them. In this way, psychologists' conclusions would be supported by layer upon layer of reliable evidence.

41

A key problem here is that humans themselves keep changing, partly in response to what psychologists have previously told them about themselves. Ask the man on the street to account for his behaviour and he may well invoke his 'unconscious' in the explanation. But before the concept of the unconscious was invented by Freud, the man would have explained himself differently.

42

The fact that fashions in psychology can change so dramatically is one more argument in Professor Parker's attack on his own profession. But whatever doubts he and those who support him hold, there is no denying the great public and media appetite for the results of even the smallest of experiments conducted by the most inexperienced of researchers.

43

There is a willing audience ready to absorb and believe things that affect all of us in our daily lives. And so without challenge, without counter-proposition, yet another rumour would enter the world of popular psychology, masquerading as proven fact.

A Although he therefore acknowledges that there have been some positive developments, Professor Parker believes there are still some very obvious problems with psychologists' techniques. An example is the temptation among university researchers to study only undergraduates.

B Psychological theories even cause people to behave differently. The agony aunts advising people on their problems in British newspapers and magazines fifty years ago absorbed the psychology of their generation and urged readers to repress feelings which they would now encourage them to indulge.

C Moreover, it is testimony to psychology's success that much of its research now appears common sense. This is because psychology's findings are more generally disseminated to a general audience than other sciences. But why is this the case?

D The week-long get-together was packed with interesting science but some of the psychology presentations were so dubious that delegates were already inclining towards his views. One researcher, for example, had discovered that impulse buyers like clothes and hi-fis but are not tempted by gardening tools or car equipment.

E But this is what Professor Parker thinks is missing: 'If the theories are built up on solid ground, the question is: where is the building? The magnificent tower of psychological knowledge never appears,' he says.

F As a result, just a day's research by a student has in the past been deemed worthy of presentation at a psychology conference. It has then duly been reported by uncritical newspapers.

G One contributing factor to this lack of academic rigour, he believes, is that the subjects who volunteer for psychology experiments are different from the rest of us. Investigations have shown that they are more insecure and they try harder to please. Indeed, they try hard to discover what result the researcher wants and then help to produce it.

H Combine this with the 'banal' or 'common sense' results that seem to flood psychology journals and conferences, and it is not surprising that the discipline of psychology may appear ridiculous to some outsiders. To restore its reputation, first and foremost psychologists must establish the foundations of their research to avoid creating a structure that rests on mere hearsay.

Test 4

Part 7

You are going to read a newspaper article about poetry. For questions **44–53**, choose from the sections (**A–D**). The sections may be chosen more than once. Mark your answers **on the separate answer sheet**.

In which section does the writer mention

the possibility of a poem following certain conventions?	44
poetry which sounds like prose?	45
particular lines of poems being precious to most people?	46
poetry being instantly recognisable?	47
evidence that poetry has long been seen as a creative act?	48
poetry being the ultimate expression of an intellectual mind?	49
professional respect for the integrity of poetry?	50
the possibility of poetry dealing with everyday matters?	51
poetry's relative lack of exposure?	52
poetry that relies for its effectiveness purely on its emotional resonance?	53

Poetry

The writer AA Gill reflects on the nature of poetry

A

One of the most satisfying things about words is their black and whiteness, the neat, austere simplicity of their process. Letters on a page are so direct and literal; you read a sentence and you can trace the thought. You know how it's done – just so long as it's prose. With poetry, however, the rules don't apply. On the face of it, it looks the same; the letters, the words, are familiar. But by some internal magic, poetry hovers above the page. It happens outside the black and white lines. Poetry is in essence a mysterious art. Poems are coded messages for your eyes only, left under pillows, tied to roses, written in water. There are no regular poetry reviews in cultural magazines, or poetry programmes on the telly. I expect Seamus Heaney and Wendy Cope could stroll hand in hand through most bookshops unmolested. Poems sell few and far, for little or less. But this reticence belies the truth of verse. Even if we haven't read a new poem for a decade, still there are verses that are the most dear cultural amulets we own, hidden in the dead letterboxes of our hearts. Snatches of verse, we take them to our end.

B

I write about 1,500 words every day. I handle them with respect and pleasure, for they are the tools of my trade. I reckon I can make a craftsman-like job of most wordy things, from a shopping list to a eulogy. But I have no idea, not the faintest inkling, of how a poem is made, and not for want of trying. Of course, I've tried. I've chopped the lines out, I've counted the syllables and made similes and metaphors, but it's barely poetry. It remains resolutely page-bound: prosaic, poetish pastiche. The hardest thing after writing poetry is writing about poetry, as you must already have noticed. It makes the author sound either pretentiously airy-fairy or thuggishly indifferent. For a start, nobody has really even satisfactorily defined what poetry is. Have a look in any dictionary, and you'll see what I mean. The word 'poet' got its first recorded use in English in the 14th century. It came from the Ancient Greek for 'the maker'. People have written books defining what poetry is and isn't, but they can only tell you the mechanics. I asked an editor what poetry was. She said, 'It's that which can't be edited.'

C

You know poetry the moment you see it; the first line tells you. Yet it has no rules. It can rhyme or not. It can have as many rhythms as a Brazilian ballroom, lines of any length, as much or as little punctuation as it feels like. But poetry can also be as rigorous as mathematics. It exists outside grammar and formula, and yet it can tie itself up in manners and etiquette. It can have any number of subtly different meanings; indeed, it can have no logical meaning at all, yet still be beautiful and touching and disturbing. A woman once wrote to Dylan Thomas saying that she loved his poetry, but was worried that her understanding of it was not what he'd intended. Thomas replied that a poem was like a city: it had many entrances.

D

I have yet to hear a convincing explanation of where poetry comes from and how it arrives, but I do know it is the highest calling of a sensitive and cerebral existence. Poetry, along with dancing and drumming is probably the most ancient of all our arts. There was rhythm and rhyme before written language. Poems lit up the memory of our collective past, told us who we were and where we came from, and they still do. People who never read poetry still reach for it at the precipitous points of their existence. At times of great happiness or terrible sadness, those places where prose is leaden with its own wordiness, only poetry will do. And there is poetry for every occasion. In my life we have had a particularly rich period of poets: Auden, Graves, Larkin, Thomas, Betjeman, to name but five. They have written between the lines on every facet of our lives, from sport to table manners. The poetry of our times is a fairer record of our concerns and hopes and our collective life than film or television or painting.

Test 4

WRITING (1 hours 30 minutes)

Part 1

Read the two texts below.

Write an essay summarising and evaluating the key points from both texts. Use your own words throughout as far as possible, and include your own ideas in your answers.

Write your answer in **240–280** words.

1

Reading Habits

For many young adults embarking on their university or college courses, reading can stop being fun and become a chore. Faced with piles of compulsory reading, it is no surprise that it loses its appeal. It is such a pity because when they were children, reading was an enormous source of pleasure, stimulating their imaginations and widening their horizons. Science fiction novels could open up the possibility of a future as a brilliant scientist, adventure stories of a dreamed-of life as an intrepid explorer. Children's choice of books often reveal their developing personalities.

Reading Aloud

Much of the pleasure of reading lies in sharing your reactions with others. I personally believe that reading aloud is a perfect pastime for all ages whether it be to a child at bedtime or an overworked and stressed adult. Listening to the written word on the radio or as a member of a book group in the company of others and discussing what you have heard is a rewarding and exhilarating experience. It allows individuals to find meaning together, to make connections and uncover memories. To put it briefly, it makes the world a better place.

Write your **essay**.

Visual materials for the Speaking test

TEST 1   **Television programme – Effects of tourism**

1A

1B

Visual materials for the Speaking test

1C

1D

Don't litter.
Preserve the natural habitat. Use trash cans and recycling bins.

TEST 2   **Magazine survey – Annoyances**

2A

2B

2C

2D

C4

Visual materials for the Speaking test

2E

2F

TEST 3 Magazine article – Sport

3A

3B

3C

Visual materials for the Speaking test

3D

3E

C7

TEST 4   Magazine article – The role of colour

4A

4B

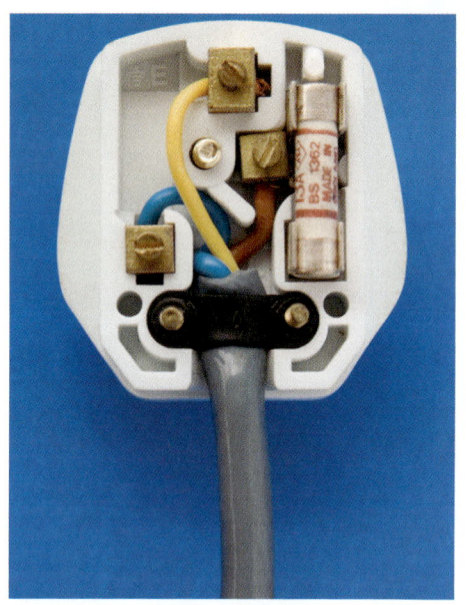

4C

Visual materials for the Speaking test

4D

4E

TEST 1

Prompt card 1a

To what extent do professional sportsmen and women need support?

- from trainers
- from the public
- from governments

TEST 2

Prompt card 2a

What creates a positive learning environment?

- people
- resources
- mood

TEST 3

Prompt card 3a

Why is it important to celebrate special dates?

- for an individual
- for a family
- for a country

TEST 4

Prompt card 4a

How much do we know about the food we eat?

- origins
- production
- labelling

TEST 1

Prompt card 1b

How important is it for effort to be recognised?
- for children
- at work
- in the arts

TEST 2

Prompt card 2b

Why do people explore the world around them?
- holidays
- business
- science

TEST 3

Prompt card 3b

How do our priorities change at different stages of life?
- relationships
- ambition
- possessions

TEST 4

Prompt card 4b

What responsibilities do governments have with regard to people's health?
- medicine
- at work
- leisure facilities

Part 2

Write an answer to **one** of the questions **2–5** in this part. Write your answer in **280–320** words in an appropriate style.

2   An international travel organisation is publishing a book entitled *Travel Changes Lives* and has asked for contributions. You decide to submit an article about a travel experience that has changed your life. You should briefly describe the experience, explain what made it so special and assess the significance of the changes in your life as a result.

   Write your **article**.

3   An English-language magazine called *International Sport* is inviting readers to write in with the name of either an individual or a team who deserve recognition for a great achievement in international sport. You decide to write a letter to the magazine with your suggestion briefly describing what was achieved, and assessing how difficult it was for the individual or team to achieve their success.

   Write your **letter**.

4   An international leisure magazine is running a series on comedy programmes shown on television around the world. It has asked readers to send in reports on comedy programmes in their countries. You decide to send in a report on a television comedy programme from your country in which you briefly describe the programme. You should also explain what it is about the characters in the programme that makes the comedy appeal to many people in your country.

   Write your **report**.

5   Write an answer to **one** of the following two questions based on **one** of the titles below. Write **5(a)** or **5(b)** at the beginning of your answer

   (a)   Marc Norman and Tom Stoppard: *Shakespeare in Love*
         A magazine has published a feature about the theme of marriage in literature. You decide to write a letter to the magazine about *Shakespeare in Love*, comparing Viola's relationships with Will and Wessex. You should also explain why Viola marries Wessex and cannot marry Will.

         Write your **letter**.

   (b)   Philip K Dick: *Do Androids Dream of Electric Sheep?*
         Your student magazine has asked for reviews of science-fiction novels. You decide to submit a review of *Do Androids Dream of Electric Sheep?* Your review should briefly explain the themes of love and loneliness in the novel with reference to Rick Deckard and John Isidore, and assess whether it is the treatment of these themes that makes the book worth reading.

         Write your **review.**

Test 4

LISTENING (40 minutes approximately)

Part 1

You will hear three different extracts.

For questions **1–6**, choose the answer (**A**, **B** or **C**) which fits best according to what you hear.

There are two questions for each extract.

Extract One

You hear Sarah Carpenter being interviewed about a campaign called Online Now, which aims to give more people in Britain access to computers.

1 Why does Sarah say she wants to increase internet use so urgently?

- **A** to improve international communication
- **B** to prevent an increase in social inequality
- **C** to involve people in economic development

2 How does Sarah say increased computer use should be achieved?

- **A** by improved access to existing facilities
- **B** by increased investment in education
- **C** by government subsidies for community centres

Extract Two

You hear a museum curator talking about one exhibit, a pestle, which was used for grinding food.

3 What does he say about the handle of the pestle?

- **A** It may originally have been designed for another purpose.
- **B** It was probably made after the ball of the pestle.
- **C** Its form is unrelated to its intended function.

4 According to the curator, what was striking about the first plants cultivated by humans?

- **A** They were all varieties of wild grasses.
- **B** They were all inedible in their natural state.
- **C** They all formed part of the diet of other animals.

Extract Three

You hear a marine biologist talking about measures to protect the oceans from pollution.

5 Why has protecting the oceans proved to be so difficult?

    A Many people do not accept that there is a serious problem.
    B The legal situation is not recognised equally around the world.
    C The activities of the fishing industry often obstruct conservation.

6 In the speaker's opinion, conservation projects that focus on individual species

    A fail to take wider implications into account.
    B cause confusion about the issues facing environmentalists.
    C provide misleading information for publication.

Test 4

Part 2

You will hear a talk about a Chinese animal called the giant panda.

For questions **7–15**, complete the sentences with a word or short phrase.

The speaker expresses surprise that the giant panda has sometimes been called a

(7) ....

The speaker says that experts sometimes regard the giant panda as a

(8) ....

The giant panda has an elongated wrist bone, which it uses like a

(9) ....

In addition to bamboo, the giant panda may eat some small creatures, as well as different types of

(10) ....

The giant panda leaves scent markings at territory boundaries which can indicate its

(11) .... as well as some physical details.

The giant panda shows hostility by making a (12) .... sound.

The giant panda now just lives in a few (13) .... regions of China.

The speaker mentions the importance of establishing areas called

(14) .... between giant panda habitats.

It has been suggested that the conservation status of the giant panda should be changed to

(15) ....

Part 3

You will hear part of a programme in which Amanda and Peter, two founders of a fruit juice company called Topfruit, talk about their business.

For questions **16–20**, choose the answer (**A**, **B**, **C** or **D**) which fits best according to what you hear.

16 What opinion is expressed about the way Topfruit was set up?
   A   It is surprising that it worked out so smoothly.
   B   Working with friends certainly saved time and energy.
   C   Having a single founder would have made the launch simpler.
   D   Since the founders had such similar views it was hard to allocate roles.

17 What is the positive culture of the company mainly attributed to?
   A   guaranteed salary increases
   B   the nature of the product that is being sold
   C   strict adherence to staff monitoring procedures
   D   certain criteria in the recruitment process

18 How do both founders feel about running their company now?
   A   They are fed up with dealing with daily problems.
   B   They feel anxious about whether its success will continue.
   C   They enjoy the challenges they face in their work.
   D   They feel pleased that they have acquired a good grasp of business.

19 When describing past mistakes in staffing, Amanda reveals
   A   her belief that good qualifications are the key factor.
   B   her acceptance that it is vital to admit failures early on.
   C   her trust that improvements can be made to the process.
   D   her fear that senior appointments are impossible to get right.

20 What gives Topfruit an advantage over its larger competitors?
   A   The emphasis on ingredients which fit market trends.
   B   The product research based on scientific models.
   C   The clarity of the labelling.
   D   The extremely sophisticated advertising.

Part 4

You will hear five short extracts in which some sportspeople are talking about their sporting successes.

TASK ONE

For questions **21–25**, choose from the list (**A–H**) what each speaker regards as the key to winning in sport.

TASK TWO

For questions **26–30**, choose from the list (**A–H**) what each speaker sees their coach as.

While you listen, you must complete both tasks.

A stamina		**A** a risk taker
B a competitive training environment	Speaker 1 [ ] 21	**B** a role model
C team spirit	Speaker 2 [ ] 22	**C** a resource
D a natural ability	Speaker 3 [ ] 23	**D** a pioneer
E attention to detail	Speaker 4 [ ] 24	**E** a motivator
F anticipation	Speaker 5 [ ] 25	**F** a traditionalist
G taking advantage of luck		**G** a disciplinarian
H intimidation		**H** a facilitator

Speaker 1 [ ] 26
Speaker 2 [ ] 27
Speaker 3 [ ] 28
Speaker 4 [ ] 29
Speaker 5 [ ] 30

SPEAKING (16 minutes)

There are two examiners. One (the interlocutor) conducts the test, providing you with the necessary materials and explaining what you have to do. The other examiner (the assessor) will be introduced to you, but then takes no further part in the interaction.

Part 1 (2 minutes)

The interlocutor first asks you and your partner a few questions which focus on information about yourselves and personal opinions.

Part 2 (4 minutes)

In this part of the test you and your partner are asked to talk together. The interlocutor places a set of pictures on the table in front of you. There may be only one picture in the set or as many as seven pictures. This stimulus provides the basis for a discussion. The interlocutor first asks an introductory question which focuses on two of the pictures (or in the case of a single picture, on aspects of the picture). After about a minute, the interlocutor gives you both a decision-making task based on the same set of pictures.

The pictures for Part 2 are on pages C8–C9 of the colour section.

Part 3 (10 minutes)

You are each given the opportunity to talk for two minutes, to comment after your partner has spoken and to take part in a more general discussion.

The interlocutor gives you a card with a question written on it and asks you to talk about it for two minutes. After you have spoken, the interlocutor asks you both another question related to the topic on the card, addressing your partner first. This procedure is repeated, so that your partner receives a card and speaks for two minutes and a follow-up question is asked.

Finally, the interlocutor asks some further questions, which leads to a discussion on a general theme related to the subjects already covered in Part 3.

The cards for Part 3 are on pages C10–C11 of the colour section.

Speaking frames

Test 1

Note: In the examination, there will be both an assessor and an interlocutor in the room.

The visual material for Part 2 is on pages C2 and C3 in the colour section of the Student's Book. The prompt cards for Part 3 are on pages C10 and C11 in the colour section of the Student's Book.

Part 1 (2 minutes / 3 minutes for groups of three)

Interlocutor: Good morning / afternoon / evening. My name is ………. and this is my colleague ………. And your names are ………. ?

Thank you.

First of all, we'd like to know something about you.

Where are you from, (Candidate A)? And you, (Candidate B)?

[address Candidate B] Are you working or studying at the moment?

[address Candidate A] And you?

Select a further question for each candidate:

- What do you enjoy about learning English?
- When do you expect to finish your studies?
- What kind of work would you like to do in the future?
- What do you like best about the area where you're living now?
- Are you living with friends or family at the moment?
- How good are you at organising your free time?

Candidates: ……………………………………………………………………

Interlocutor: Thank you.

Part 2 (approximately 4 minutes / 6 minutes for groups of three)   *Television programme – Effects of tourism*

Interlocutor: Now, in this part of the test you're going to do something together. Here are some pictures taken by people on holiday.

*Place picture sheet for Test 1 (pages C2 and C3) in front of the candidates. Select **two** of the pictures for the candidates to look at*.*

First, I'd like you to look at pictures * and * and talk together about the kind of holidays these pictures suggest.

88

Speaking frames

You have about a minute for this, so don't worry if I interrupt you.

(*2 minutes for groups of three*)

Candidates:
⏲ *1 minute*
(*2 minutes for groups of three*) ....

Interlocutor: Thank you. Now look at all the pictures.

I'd like you to imagine that there's going to be a television programme about the effects tourists can have on the places they visit.

Talk together about the different effects of tourism suggested by the pictures. Then decide which issue should be highlighted in the first programme.

You have about three minutes to talk about this. (*4 minutes for groups of three*)

Candidates:
⏲ *3 minutes*
(*4 minutes for groups of three*) ....

Interlocutor: Thank you. *Retrieve picture sheet.*

Part 3 (approximately 10 minutes)   *Recognition*

Interlocutor: Now, in this part of the test you're each going to talk on your own for about two minutes. You need to listen while your partner is speaking because you'll be asked to comment afterwards.

So, (*Candidate A*), I'm going to give you a card with a question written on it and I'd like you to tell us what you think. There are also some ideas on the card for you to use if you like.

All right? Here is your card, and a copy for you (*Candidate B*).

Hand over a copy of prompt card 1a (page C10) to both candidates.

Remember (*Candidate A*), you have about two minutes to talk before we join in.

[*Allow up to 10 seconds before saying, if necessary:* Would you like to begin now?]

Candidate A: ....
⏲ *2 minutes*

Interlocutor: Thank you.

Interlocutor: *Ask one of the following questions to Candidate B:*

Speaking frames

- Should a nation's sportsmen and women be valued as highly as people working in business?
- Do you agree that some sports stars are paid too much?
- Which is more important, taking part or winning?

> *Invite Candidate A to join in by selecting one of the following prompts:*
>
> - What do you think?
> - Do you agree?
> - How about you?

Candidates:
🕐 *1 minute* ....

Interlocutor: Thank you. *Retrieve cards.*

Interlocutor: Now (*Candidate B*), it's your turn to be given a question. Here is your card, and a copy for you (*Candidate A*).

Hand over a copy of prompt card 1b (page C11) to both candidates.

Remember (*Candidate B*), you have about two minutes to tell us what you think, and there are some ideas on the card for you to use if you like. All right?

[*Allow up to 10 seconds before saying, if necessary:* Would you like to begin now?]

Candidate B:
🕐 *2 minutes* ....

Interlocutor: Thank you.

Interlocutor: *Ask one of the following questions to Candidate A:*

- If you could win a prize or award for doing something, what would it be for?
- In what ways, other than with money, can employers effectively show their appreciation for work well done?
- To what extent are you motivated by praise?

> *Invite Candidate B to join in by selecting one of the following prompts:*
>
> - What do you think?
> - Do you agree?
> - How about you?

Candidates:
🕐 *1 minute* ....

Interlocutor: Thank you. *Retrieve cards.*

Interlocutor:	Now, to finish the test, we're going to talk about 'recognition' in general.
	Address a selection of the following questions to both candidates: • Why do some people seek public recognition while others prefer to avoid it? • In your country, what are the recognised signs of success? • How important do you think award ceremonies really are? • Should important people have streets or public places named after them? .... (Why? / Why not?) • In your opinion, is there any area of human achievement which deserves to be more publicly recognised? • Some people say criticism can be more useful than praise. What's your opinion?
Candidates:	……………………………………………………………............………

🕐 *up to 4 minutes*

Interlocutor:	Thank you. That is the end of the test.

Speaking frames

Test 2

Note: In the examination, there will be both an assessor and an interlocutor in the room.

The visual material for Part 2 is on pages C4 and C5 in the colour section of the Student's Book. The prompt cards for Part 3 are on pages C10 and C11 in the colour section of the Student's Book.

Part 1 (2 minutes / 3 minutes for groups of three)

Interlocutor:	Good morning / afternoon / evening. My name is ………. and this is my colleague ………. And your names are ………. ?
	Thank you.
	First of all, we'd like to know something about you.
	Where are you from, (Candidate A)? And you, (Candidate B)?
	[*address Candidate B*] Are you working or studying at the moment?
	[*address Candidate A*] And you?
	Select a further question for each candidate:
	• What do you enjoy about learning English? • When do you expect to finish your studies? • What kind of work would you like to do in the future? • What do you like best about the area where you're living now? • Are you living with friends or family at the moment? • How good are you at organising your free time?
Candidates:	……………………………………………………………………………
Interlocutor:	Thank you.

Part 2 (approximately 4 minutes /   *Magazine survey – Annoyances*
6 minutes for groups of three)

Interlocutor:	Now, in this part of the test you're going to do something together. Here are some pictures of different situations.
	*Place picture sheet for Test 2 (pages C4 and C5) in front of the candidates. Select **two** of the pictures for the candidates to look at*.*
	First, I'd like you to look at pictures * and * and talk together about what sounds you associate with these situations.
	You have about a minute for this, so don't worry if I interrupt you. (*2 minutes for groups of three*)

Candidates:
⏱ *1 minute*
(2 minutes for
groups of three) …………………………………………………………………

92

Speaking frames

Interlocutor:	Thank you. Now look at all the pictures.
	I'd like you to imagine a magazine is doing a survey on things that annoy us.
	Talk together about how these annoyances affect different individuals. Then decide which annoyance has the biggest impact on society.
	You have about three minutes to talk about this. (*4 minutes for groups of three*)

Candidates:
⏱ *3 minutes*
(*4 minutes for groups of three*) ....

Interlocutor:	Thank you. *Retrieve picture sheet.*

Part 3 (approximately 10 minutes)   *Surroundings*

Interlocutor:	Now, in this part of the test you're each going to talk on your own for about two minutes. You need to listen while your partner is speaking because you'll be asked to comment afterwards.
	So (*Candidate A*), I'm going to give you a card with a question written on it and I'd like you to tell us what you think. There are also some ideas on the card for you to use if you like.
	All right? Here is your card, and a copy for you (*Candidate B*).
	Hand over a copy of prompt card 2a (page C10) to both candidates.
	Remember (*Candidate A*), you have about two minutes to talk before we join in.
	[*Allow up to 10 seconds before saying, if necessary:* Would you like to begin now?]

Candidate A:
⏱ *2 minutes* ....

Interlocutor:	Thank you.
Interlocutor:	Ask **one** of the following questions to Candidate B:
	• Do you think that schools do a good job? • Do you learn better in calm or lively surroundings? .... (Why is that?) • How can class size affect learning?

93

Speaking frames

	Invite Candidate A to join in by selecting one of the following prompts: • What do you think? • Do you agree? • How about you?
Candidates: 🕓 *1 minute*	....
Interlocutor:	Thank you. *Retrieve cards.*
Interlocutor:	Now (*Candidate B*), it's your turn to be given a question. Here is your card, and a copy for you (*Candidate A*). *Hand over a copy of prompt card 2b (page C11) to both candidates.* Remember (*Candidate B*), you have about two minutes to tell us what you think, and there are some ideas on the card for you to use if you like. All right? [*Allow up to 10 seconds before saying, if necessary:* Would you like to begin now?]
Candidate B: 🕓 *2 minutes*	....
Interlocutor:	Thank you.
Interlocutor:	*Ask* **one** *of the following questions to Candidate A:* • Would you enjoy a job that involved a lot of travelling? .... (Why? / Why not?) • Why do you think some people prefer not to travel long distances? • If you visited a new place, which would interest you more, the people or the sights?
	Invite Candidate B to join in by selecting one of the following prompts: • What do you think? • Do you agree? • How about you?
Candidates: 🕓 *1 minute*	....
Interlocutor:	Thank you. *Retrieve cards.*
Interlocutor:	Now, to finish the test, we're going to talk about 'surroundings' in general. *Address a selection of the following questions to both candidates:* • What can you learn about a person by looking at their work-space?

- What skills should children be taught to prepare them for the world around them?
- Should companies be allowed to advertise their products in schools? ………. (Why? / Why not?)
- What is your attitude towards keeping animals in zoos and wildlife parks?
- What do you think makes a good neighbourhood?
- How can new experiences change your ideas about the way you live?

Candidates: ……………………………………………………………………

🕐 *up to 4 minutes*

Interlocutor: Thank you. That is the end of the test.

Speaking frames

Test 3

Note: In the examination, there will be both an assessor and an interlocutor in the room.

The visual material for Part 2 is on pages C6 and C7 in the colour section of the Student's Book. The prompt cards for Part 3 are on pages C10 and C11 in the colour section of the Student's Book.

Part 1 (2 minutes / 3 minutes for groups of three)

Interlocutor: Good morning / afternoon / evening. My name is ………. and this is my colleague ……… And your names are ……….. ?

Thank you.

First of all, we'd like to know something about you.

Where are you from, (Candidate A)? And you, (Candidate B)?

[*address Candidate B*] Are you working or studying at the moment?

[*address Candidate A*] And you?

Select a further question for each candidate:

- What do you enjoy about learning English?
- When do you expect to finish your studies?
- What kind of work would you like to do in the future?
- What do you like best about the area where you're living now?
- Are you living with friends or family at the moment?
- How good are you at organising your free time?

Candidates: ……………………………………………………………………………

Interlocutor: Thank you.

Part 2 (approximately 4 minutes / 6 minutes for groups of three)   *Magazine article – Sport*

Interlocutor: Now, in this part of the test you're going to do something together. Here are some pictures of different aspects of sport.

*Place picture sheet for Test 3 (pages C6 and C7) in front of the candidates. Select **two** of the pictures for the candidates to look at*.*

First, I'd like you to look at pictures * and * and talk together about how you think the people might be feeling.

You have about a minute for this, so don't worry if I interrupt you. *(2 minutes for groups of three)*

Candidates:
⏲ *1 minute*
(2 minutes for groups of three) ……………………………………………………………

96

Speaking frames

Interlocutor:	Thank you. Now look at all the pictures.
	I'd like you to imagine that a magazine is planning an article on the influence of sport on people's lives today and needs two photographs to illustrate the article.
	Talk together about the influences of sport on people's lives, as shown by these photographs. Then decide which two would be best to illustrate the article.
	You have about three minutes to talk about this. (*4 minutes for groups of three*)
Candidates: ⏱ *3 minutes* (*4 minutes for groups of three*)	....
Interlocutor:	Thank you. *Retrieve picture sheet.*

Part 3 (approximately 10 minutes)   *Special times*

Interlocutor:	Now, in this part of the test you're each going to talk on your own for about two minutes. You need to listen while your partner is speaking because you'll be asked to comment afterwards.
	So (*Candidate A*), I'm going to give you a card with a question written on it and I'd like you to tell us what you think. There are also some ideas on the card for you to use if you like.
	All right? Here is your card, and a copy for you (*Candidate B*).
	Hand over a copy of prompt card 3a (page C10) to both candidates.
	Remember (*Candidate A*), you have about two minutes to talk before we join in.
	[*Allow up to 10 seconds before saying, if necessary:* Would you like to begin now?]
Candidate A: ⏱ *2 minutes*	....
Interlocutor:	Thank you.
Interlocutor:	*Ask **one** of the following questions to Candidate B:*
	• Do you prefer national or personal celebrations? .... (Why?) • What have you celebrated recently? • What is the most important occasion in a person's life in your country?

> *Invite Candidate A to join in by selecting one of the following prompts:*
>
> • What do you think?
> • Do you agree?
> • How about you?

Speaking frames

Candidates: ⏱ 1 minute	....
Interlocutor:	Thank you. *Retrieve cards.*
Interlocutor:	Now (*Candidate B*), it's your turn to be given a question. Here is your card, and a copy for you (*Candidate A*).
	Hand over a copy of prompt card 3b (page C11) to both candidates.
	Remember (*Candidate B*), you have about two minutes to tell us what you think, and there are some ideas on the card for you to use if you like. All right?
	[*Allow up to 10 seconds before saying, if necessary:* Would you like to begin now?]
Candidate B: ⏱ 2 minutes	....
Interlocutor:	Thank you.
Interlocutor:	*Ask one of the following questions to Candidate A:*

- Is it good for us to always get what we want? .... (Why? / Why not?)
- At what age should people retire? .... (Why?)
- Which of your possessions do you value most? .... (Why?)

> *Invite Candidate B to join in by selecting one of the following prompts:*
> - What do you think?
> - Do you agree?
> - How about you?

Candidates: ⏱ 1 minute	....
Interlocutor:	Thank you. *Retrieve cards.*
Interlocutor:	Now, to finish the test, we're going to talk about 'special times' in general.
	Address a selection of the following questions to both candidates:

- Which is the more significant event, starting school or leaving school?
- There's a saying that schooldays are the happiest days of your life. What do you think?
- Why do many people find historical events interesting?
- Do you feel that there are the right number of public holidays in your country? .... (Why? / Why not?)
- Why do some people say that a new year is a new beginning?
- What makes one occasion more memorable than another?

Candidates: ⏱ up to 4 minutes	....
Interlocutor:	Thank you. That is the end of the test.

Test 4

Note: In the examination, there will be both an assessor and an interlocutor in the room.

The visual material for Part 2 is on pages C8 and C9 in the colour section of the Student's Book. The prompt cards for Part 3 are on pages C10 and C11 in the colour section of the Student's Book.

Part 1 (2 minutes / 3 minutes for groups of three)

Interlocutor: Good morning / afternoon / evening. My name is .... and this is my colleague .... And your names are .... ?

Thank you.

First of all, we'd like to know something about you.

Where are you from, (Candidate A)? And you, (Candidate B)?

[*address Candidate B*] Are you working or studying at the moment?

[*address Candidate A*] And you?

Select a further question for each candidate:

- What do you enjoy about learning English?
- When do you expect to finish your studies?
- What kind of work would you like to do in the future?
- What do you like best about the area where you're living now?
- Are you living with friends or family at the moment?
- How good are you at organising your free time?

Candidates: ....

Interlocutor: Thank you.

Part 2 (approximately 4 minutes / 6 minutes for groups of three)   *Magazine article – The role of colour*

Interlocutor: Now, in this part of the test you're going to do something together. Here are some pictures on the theme of colour.

*Place picture sheet for Test 4 (C8 and C9) in front of the candidates. Select **two** of the pictures for the candidates to look at*.*

First, I'd like you to look at pictures * and * and talk together about why these pictures might have been taken.

You have about a minute for this, so don't worry if I interrupt you. (*2 minutes for groups of three*)

Candidates:
⏱ *1 minute*
(*2 minutes for groups of three*) ....

99

Speaking frames

Interlocutor:	Thank you. Now look at all the pictures.
	I'd like you to imagine that a magazine is publishing an article on the role of colour in people's lives.
	Talk together about how the pictures illustrate the importance of colour. Then decide which two pictures represent the <u>least</u> important roles of colour and should not accompany the article.
	You have about three minutes to talk about this. (*4 minutes for groups of three*)
Candidates: 🕐 3 minutes (*4 minutes for groups of three*)	....
Interlocutor:	Thank you. *Retrieve the picture sheet.*

Part 3 (approximately 10 minutes)   *Health*

Interlocutor:	Now, in this part of the test you're each going to talk on your own for about two minutes. You need to listen while your partner is speaking because you'll be asked to comment afterwards.
	So (*Candidate A*), I'm going to give you a card with a question written on it and I'd like you to tell us what you think. There are also some ideas on the card for you to use if you like.
	All right? Here is your card, and a copy for you (*Candidate B*).
	Hand over a copy of prompt card 4a (page C10) to both candidates.
	Remember (*Candidate A*), you have about two minutes to talk before we join in.
	[*Allow up to 10 seconds before saying, if necessary:* Would you like to begin now?]
Candidate A: 🕐 2 minutes	....
Interlocutor:	Thank you.
Interlocutor:	*Ask one of the following questions to Candidate B:*
	• Why do you think ready-made food is so popular? • What's the value of teaching children cookery skills in schools? • The number of vegetarians is increasing. Why do you think this is?

> *Invite Candidate A to join in by selecting one of the following prompts:*
>
> • What do you think?
> • Do you agree?
> • How about you?

Speaking frames

Candidates: ⏱ 1 minute	....
Interlocutor:	Thank you. *Retrieve cards.*
Interlocutor:	Now (*Candidate B*), it's your turn to be given a question. Here is your card, and a copy for you (*Candidate A*). *Hand over a copy of prompt card 4b (page C11) to both candidates.* Remember (*Candidate B*), you have about two minutes to tell us what you think, and there are some ideas on the card for you to use if you like. All right? [*Allow up to 10 seconds before saying, if necessary:* Would you like to begin now?]
Candidate B: ⏱ 2 minutes	....
Interlocutor:	Thank you.
Interlocutor:	*Ask **one** of the following questions to Candidate A:* • How do you think health services should be financed? • Are doctors respected in your/this country? • What's your opinion of banning smoking in public places? > *Invite Candidate B to join in by selecting one of the following prompts:* > > • What do you think? > • Do you agree? > • How about you?
Candidates: ⏱ 1 minute	....
Interlocutor:	Thank you. Retrieve cards.
Interlocutor:	Now, to finish the test, we're going to talk about 'health' in general. *Address a selection of the following questions to both candidates:* • Research says all five senses are involved in the enjoyment of a meal. How important do you think this is? • What do you understand by the term 'alternative medicine'? .... (How effective is it, in your view?) • It is said that laughter is the best medicine. What do you think about this? • Do you think celebrities set a good example in terms of health? .... (Why? / Why not?) • What do you think is the healthiest form of exercise? .... (Why?) • What problems will we face because people are living longer?
Candidates: up to ⏱ 4 minutes	....
Interlocutor:	Thank you. That is the end of the test.

Marks and results

Reading and Use of English

One mark is given for each correct answer in Parts 1–3 and 7. Two marks are given for each correct answer for Parts 5–6. Up to two marks are awarded for Part 4. The total score is then weighted to 80 marks for the whole Reading and Use of English paper.

Writing assessment

Examiners mark tasks using Assessment Scales that were developed with explicit reference to the Common European Framework of Reference for Languages (CEFR). The scales, which are used across the spectrum of Cambridge ESOL's General and Business English Writing tests, consist of four subscales: Content, Communicative Achievement, Organisation, and Language:

Content focuses on how well the candidate has fulfilled the task, in other words if they have done what they were asked to do.

Communicative Achievement focuses on how appropriate the writing is for the task and whether the candidate has used the appropriate register.

Organisation focuses on the way the candidate puts together the piece of writing, in other words if it is logical and ordered.

Language focuses on vocabulary and grammar. This includes the range of language as well as how accurate it is.

Responses are marked on each subscale from 0 to 5. The subscale Content is common to all levels:

	Content
5	All content is relevant to the task. Target reader is fully informed.
3	Minor irrelevances and/or omissions may be present. Target reader is on the whole informed.
1	Irrelevances and misinterpretation of task may be present. Target reader is minimally informed.
0	Content is totally irrelevant Target reader is not informed.

The remaining three subscales (Communicative Achievement, Organisation, and Language) have descriptors specific to each CEFR level:

Marks and results

CEFR level	Communicative Achievement	Organisation	Language
C2	Uses the conventions of the communicative task with sufficient flexibility to communicate complex ideas in an effective way, holding the target reader's attention with ease, fulfilling all communicative purposes.	Text is organised impressively and coherently using a wide range of cohesive devices and organisational patterns with complete flexibility.	Uses a wide range of vocabulary, including less common lexis, with fluency, precision, sophistication and style. Use of grammar is sophisticated, fully controlled and completely neutral. Any inaccuracies occur only as slips.
C1	Uses the conventions of the communicative task effectively to hold the target reader's attention and communicate straightforward and complex ideas, as appropriate.	Text is a well-organised, coherent whole, using a variety of cohesive devices and organisational patterns with flexibility.	Uses a range of vocabulary, including less common lexis, appropriately. Uses a range of simple and complex grammatical forms with control and flexibility. Occasional errors may be present but do not impede communication.
B2	Uses the conventions of the communicative task to hold the target reader's attention and communicate straightforward ideas.	Text is generally well organised and coherent, using a variety of linking words and cohesive devices.	Uses a range of everyday vocabulary appropriately, with occasional inappropriate use of less common lexis. Uses a range of simple and some complex grammatical forms with a good degree of control. Errors do not impede communication.
B1	Uses the conventions of the communicative task in generally appropriate ways to communicate straightforward ideas.	Text is connected and coherent, using basic linking words and a limited number of cohesive devices.	Uses everyday vocabulary generally appropriately, while occasionally overusing certain lexis. Uses simple grammatical forms with a good degree of control. While errors are noticeable, meaning can still be determined.
A2	Produces text that communicates simple ideas in simple ways.	Text is connected using basic, high-frequency linking words.	Uses basic vocabulary reasonably appropriately. Uses simple grammatical forms with some degree of control. Errors may impede meaning at times.

Marks and results

CPE Writing Examiners use the following Assessment Scale, extracted from the one above:

C2	Content	Communicative Achievement	Organisation	Language
5	All content is relevant to the task. Target reader is fully informed.	Demonstrates complete command of the conventions of the communicative task. Communicates complex ideas in an effective and convincing way, holding the target reader's attention with ease, fulfilling all communicative purposes.	Text is organised impressively and coherently using a wide range of cohesive devices and organisational patterns with complete flexibility.	Uses a wide range of vocabulary, including less common lexis, with fluency, precision, sophistication, and style. Use of grammar is sophisticated, fully controlled and completely natural. Any inaccuracies occur only as slips.
4	*Performance shares features of Bands 3 and 5.*			
3	Minor irrelevances and/or omissions may be present. Target reader is on the whole informed.	Uses the conventions of the communicative task with sufficient flexibility to communicate complex ideas in an effective way, holding the target reader's attention with ease, fulfilling all communicative purposes.	Text is a well-organised, coherent whole, using a variety of cohesive devices and organisational patterns with flexibility.	Uses a range of vocabulary, including less common lexis, effectively and precisely. Uses a wide range of simple and complex grammatical forms with full control, flexibility and sophistication. Errors, if present, are related to less common words and structures, or as slips.
2	*Performance shares features of Bands 1 and 3.*			
1	Irrelevances and misinterpretation of task may be present. Target reader is minimally informed.	Uses the conventions of the communicative task effectively to hold the target reader's attention and communicate straightforward and complex ideas, as appropriate.	Text is well organised and coherent, using a variety of cohesive devices and organisational patterns to generally good effect.	Uses a range of vocabulary, including less common lexis, appropriately. Uses a range of simple and complex grammatical forms with control and flexibility. Occasional errors may be present but do not impede communication.
0	Content is totally irrelevant. Target reader is not informed.	*Performance below Band 1.*		

When marking the tasks, examiners take into account length of responses. Scripts which are under- or over-length are not penalised *per se*. Responses which are too short may not have an adequate range of language and may not provide all the information that is required, while responses which are too long may contain irrelevant content and have a negative effect on the reader. These factors may affect candidates' marks on the relevant subscales.

Paper 2 sample answers and examiner's comments

The following pieces of writing have been selected from students' answers. The samples relate to tasks in Tests 1–4. Explanatory notes have been added to show how the bands have been arrived at. The comments on Part 1 questions and Part 2 questions 5a and 5b should be read in conjunction with the Briefing Documents included in the Keys.

Marks and results

Sample A (Test 1, Part 2, Question 4, Report)

This report is written in order to provide an overview of the public park located in the centre of the town. Another aim of this report is to suggest desirable improvements to the existing facilities and the general state of park and explain why visitors would be attracted.

General overview

The park in question was designed in 1980 in order to develop a recreational area for the neighbouring households as well as to provide local children with appropriate sports and leasure facilities. Since then, very little developments have been carried out. Currently, the park offers its visitors two playgrounds for pre-school/schoolchildren, one football pitch and two cafés, one of which is a well-known fast-food brand.

Proposed improvements

Although the general state of the park could be considered satisfactory, there is still room for improvement.

In terms of sports facilities, a dire need for winter sports is obvious. One of the options would be building an ice-rink for the winter time, when general public normally lose interest in sports such as football.

Alternately, an enclosed volleyball/basketball playground could be considered.

As for the food establishments, it is clear that the park definitely lacks catering for people with special diets. Not only does it not offer vegetarian menu, there is also no possibility for young mothers to feed their babies/toddlers properly.

I would recommend the local government pay closer attention to this issue and consider opening new cafés/restaurants with these customer groups in view.

Conclusion

In conclusion, I would like highlight the importance of improving the park's facilities. Not only does the park already provide local people with opportunities for healthy lifestyle, the new improvements suggested would also create an image of the town as a friendly, open place with a welcoming, relaxed atmosphere for different people all year round.

Subscale	Mark	Commentary
Content	5	All content is relevant to the task and the target reader would be informed as to the facilities the park offers and would know what improvements are being proposed. The final part of the question is dealt with, although not a great amount of detail is provided.
Communicative Achievement	3	The candidate uses the conventions of a report with a degree of flexibility thereby communicating complex ideas in an effective way, holding the target reader's attention with ease and fulfilling all communicative purposes. An appropriate formal register is used throughout the report (*another aim of this report is to suggest desirable improvements to the existing facilities and the general state of the park ..., Although the general state of the park could be considered satisfactory, there is still room for improvement, In conclusion I would like highlight the importance of improving the park's facilities*). The format is also appropriate with clear and helpful headings.
Organisation	2	The text is a well-organised, coherent whole, using a variety of cohesive devices and organisational patterns with flexibility. This ranges from simpler linking words and phrases (*there is also, as well as, although*) to more complex cohesive devices and organisational patterns (*in terms of, as for, the park in question, one of which, not only does it ... there is also, it is clear that ...*). However, there are instances of incorrectly used cohesive devices (*alternately*).
Language	3	A range of vocabulary, including less common lexis, is used effectively and precisely (*pay closer attention to this issue, highlight the importance of, room for improvement, catering for, provide an overview*) but some vocabulary is not used appropriately or accurately (*in view, dire need*). A wide range of simple and complex grammatical forms is used with control and some flexibility. There are some examples of grammatical error which do not impede (*This report is written ..., very little developments*) and may only be slips.

Marks and results

Sample B (Test 2, Part 1, Question 1, Essay)

The expression of diametrically opposed opinions has always been a great tool in the arsenal of journalists, especially film critics. One can easily be swayed to vouch for either side, especially if there are questions of loyalty or fundamental ideological values involved. This can be seen in the very polarised stance expressed either in favour of the position that film in the 21st century as an art or entertainment form is in decline or in the hope that it has and will always keep its hold on audiences as one of the most immediate and powerful means of moulding public awareness of social and moral issues.

Yet it might only be a question of differentiation of purposes, audience needs to create different styles of film for well-defined audiences (children, teenagers, lovers of great classics from the 20s or 50s say, advocates of social realism, fans of horror, and so on), with precise budgets and therefore well-aimed marketing strategies. Perhaps the film industry has finally come of age and can deliver well-groomed 'horses' for better known 'courses', as the saying goes. There is nobody who is forcing the wrong people to go and see either a blockbuster in a multiplex cinema with an audience of popcorn-eating spotty bored teenagers for whom going to see an action movie might well be an escape from dreariness and monotony of their everyday lives as they see it. Equally, there is no authority to make people pay for a low budget thought-provoking film in an art picturehouse if that does not appeal to them. There is always choice involved, and that is what any human art form has retained as one of its fundamental values. Besides, this does not preclude that, from time-to-time, major films with a big budget cannot manage to appeal to more layers of the target audience than just one. Similarly, not all low-budget movies are valuable in terms of artistry, still, originality or novelty of ideas they build on. Each film should be appreciated in its own context, and that way modern classics can be identified and treated equally.

Film will – hopefully – always stay around and diversify in its use of new technologies or age-old techniques, its themes and genres (be they comedies, documentaries, historical dramas, or science fiction or whatever) and its use of professionals' skills and artistry. That way audiences will always be able to exercise their vote by choosing what to go and see next at the pictures, and extreme opinion on the decline or otherwise of the greatest art form we have can be held at bay.

Subscale	Mark	Commentary
Content*	5	All content is relevant to the task. The target reader is fully informed. The essay does not merely work through the key points one by one, but skilfully incorporates them in an essay which is principally focused on eloquently expressing the writer's strong views on modern cinema, rather than simply restating the arguments in the two texts.
Communicative Achievement	5	The text demonstrates a complete command of the conventions of an essay. The opening paragraph clearly sets out the approach the writer is going to take, and the final paragraph is an effective and appropriate conclusion which does more than simply restate the writer's earlier views, and is a natural development of the arguments made earlier in the essay. Complex ideas about the cinema and the attitudes people have to it are communicated in an effective and often very convincing way, holding the target reader's attention with ease and fulfilling all communicative purposes.
Organisation	4	The essay is a very well-organised and coherent whole, and uses a good variety of cohesive devices and organisational patterns with a good degree of flexibility (*This can be seen in …, Similarly, Besides, Equally, Yet it might only be a question of …*).
Language	4	A wide range of vocabulary, including less common lexis, is used with fluency, precision and some sophistication (*diametrically opposed, a great tool in the arsenal of journalists, easily be swayed, has finally come of age, dreariness and monotony, diversify, held at bay*). There are occasional minor slips or examples of slight awkwardness (*it does not preclude that …, exercise their vote, not all low-budget movies are valuable in terms of artistry, still, originality or novelty of ideas they build on.*).

* See Briefing Document, pages 132–133. Key points from each Part 1 question are listed in a Briefing Document for markers.

Marks and results

Sample C (Test 2, Part 2, Question 4, Review)

Talk-Talk is a piece of PC software designed to exchange messages between computer users. When registering, the users are issued with a number, which is their log-in and, at the same time, their contact number.

Talk-Talk is a tiny programme, capable of doing big things! Apart from being able to exchange pieces of textual information, the software allows its users to send text messages to each others' mobile numbers, do voice calls, record voice messages and even send files – including photos.

Since its introduction in the 1990s, the programme had only gained new fans and the company owning it has made a lot of profit through adverts. So what is the secret of Talk-Talk's success?

First and foremost – it allows users to contact each other instantly and with practically no costs (apart from the cost of electricity needed for running the PC). Secondly, Talk-Talk is absolutely free. Computer owners can just download the full version from the website, or simply copy the file from their friend's machine. The file itself does not weigh much which adds to the benefits of the user. Furthermore, the programme's interface is really straightforward and the information architecture is easy to follow. The icons and text can be reduced or enlarged in size and the colours of the interface are changeable, which greatly adds to Talk-Talk's appeal to users across all generations. Last, but not least, the programme allows users to engage in a range of social situations with its wide variety of features including picture sharing, text messaging and voice calling, just to name a few.

Talk-Talk clearly distinguishes itself from similar programmes with its broad functionality, easiness of use and efficiency of messaging. And all of this for free!

Marks and results

Subscale	Mark	Commentary
Content	5	All content is relevant to the task and the target reader would be fully informed as to what the technological innovation is, what it can do and the reasons for its popularity. The final point is dealt with in some detail with four different reasons clearly presented.
Communicative Achievement	3	The candidate uses the conventions of a review effectively and with some flexibility to communicate complex ideas, holding the target reader's attention with ease, fulfilling all communicative purposes. The review begins somewhat abruptly, but has an appropriate, though brief, concluding paragraph which would be effective in persuading the reader to purchase the product.
Organisation	3	The review is well-organised and coherent using a variety of cohesive devices and organisational patterns to good effect (*apart from being …, Since its introduction, First and foremost, So what is the secret of Talk-Talk's success?*). The review is clearly organised into five paragraphs, though in the fourth paragraph the points are dealt with somewhat mechanically (*Secondly, … Furthermore, … Last, but not least*).
Language	2	A range of vocabulary, including less common lexis essential when talking about technology, is used both effectively and precisely (*issued with a number, download the full version, engage in a range of social activities, the programme's interface, information architecture, clearly distinguishes itself from*). A range of simple and complex grammatical forms is used with full control and flexibility. Errors are present but are probably slips (*easiness of use, the programme had only gained new fans*).

Sample D (Test 3, Part 1, Question 1, Essay)

Home-made food vs convenience food

The speed of modern life makes people forget about simple things like sitting round the table with the family, chatting, sharing experiences of the day while enjoying delicious home-made meal. It's far too faster and more convenient to grab something from the shelf in the supermarket and just to put into the microwave oven to be ready in 5 minutes. It goes without saying that it saves time, energy and effort for a person under constant pressure of his work. It also gives you an opportunity to try the variety of dishes you'll never be able to cook at home. But an important question to consider is whether such food can be considered healthy enough and whether you are prepared to take the risk of feeding your children with such variety of food and treating indigestion later. Can anything be compared with the satisfaction a young mother has from a grateful child eating everything she has just cooked and asking for another helping. It's the essence of our maternal/paternal love showing care with simple things. Moreover, on a personal level, the process of cooking is creation of something new when people change the flavour with a new touch here or there that brings real satisfaction and increase your self-esteem. It adds to the attraction of the house if your guests are treated to home-made food prepared with care and affection. The food served, the whole atmosphere triggers a friendly conversation round the table.

Besides, culinary traditions can be an idea to unite the nation. It's "borsch" that the Ukrainians traditionally are extremely proud of. And in any corner of the world a true Ukrainian will treat you to this national dish. And in turn he will be treated to a different dish which is served in these parts and thus a new friendship starts.

So food is not a simple common thing that is a part of our everyday life, it's something more complex and deep that influences every sphere of people's being beginning from health and ending with inner psychological processes.

It's a notion that can't be evaluated but only appreciated

Subscale	Mark	Commentary
Content*	5	All content is relevant to the task. The target reader would be fully informed as all four key points are included in the essay and there is also some development of each point.
Communicative Achievement	2	The conventions of the essay are used effectively to hold the target reader's attention and communicate straightforward and complex ideas with some ease, fulfilling all communicative purposes. The essay lacks an introduction and starts quite abruptly by addressing the first key point, although the conclusion is more effective (even if the paragraphing is not correct). The register is consistently appropriate for an essay.
Organisation	1	The text is well-organised and coherent, using a variety of cohesive devices and organisational patterns to generally good effect (*It goes without saying …, Moreover, But an important question to consider is …, and thus …*). In a few cases cohesive devices are not used wholly appropriately or effectively (*Besides, So*) and some are over-used (*And*). Clear paragraphs are used, though the first one is over-long and the last two should be combined.
Language	2	The candidate uses a range of vocabulary, including less common lexis, appropriately and sometimes quite precisely and effectively (*inner psychological processes, treating indigestion, it's the essence of our maternal / paternal love, increase your self-esteem*). A range of simple and complex grammatical forms are used with control and flexibility. There are very occasional errors which do not impede communication (*It's far too faster, such variety of food, sharing experiences of the day while enjoying delicious home-made meal*).

* See Briefing Document, page 141. Key points from each Part 1 question are listed in a Briefing Document for markers.

Marks and results

Sample E (Test 4, Part 2, Question 2, Article)

It is an absolute truth that travel changes lives, and I would like to recount my own story about a change that took place in my life due to a great travel I did to Israel.

Before embarking on this trip, my mind was always judgemental about the bellic actions taken by The Jews against the Arabs and the same thing the other way around.

According to the severity of the war actions taken I used to side with one or the other, but now that I have seen, with my own eyes, the way in which Jews and Arabs share, though in a tense ambiance, the city of Tel-Aviv, I can state, with most certainty, that both the Palestinians, as well as the Jews, deserve to live in a peaceful manner because everybody is entitled to a happy life, to raise a family and to grow up as an accomplished human being.

I remember watching two moms walking down the street pushing their baby carts, one beside the other, one of them was dressed as a Jewish woman and the other lady wore a Muslim attire. I saw them walking side by side on the streets of Tel-Aviv and I thought to myself 'Don't they both deserve or have the right to enjoy their city without the fear and the constant threat of an unexpected attack? Who is right? Who is wrong? They are both right and wrong.

This experience on the streets of Tel-Aviv was so special to me, because it made me think of my good and tranquil childhood, compared to that of the Jewish and Muslim children in Israel.

I also came to realize that most of the news programs are biased regarding their national interests and the way they want to influence people's opinions. But, not until one sees with one's own eyes what the situations really are, one comes to the conclusion that life is much more complex than one could ever think. But in order to see, one has to travel. Most definitely, travel changes lives.

Subscale	Mark	Commentary
Content	4	All content is relevant to the task and the target reader is informed. The analysis of the significance of the changes in the writer's life as a result of their travel experience lacks detailed development, but the point is dealt with quite well.
Communicative Achievement	1	The writer uses the conventions of the article effectively to hold the target reader's attention and communicate straightforward and complex ideas, as appropriate. The introductory sentence and the concluding sentence are reasonably effective but not particularly engaging or original ways of starting and finishing an article.
Organisation	2	The text is well-organised and coherent, using a variety of cohesive devices and organisational patterns to generally good effect (*Before embarking, but now I have seen the way in which …, This experience … was special because …, compared to that of, But in order to see, I also came to realise that …*). There are instances where ambition in this area is not completely successful (*But, not until one sees … One comes to the conclusion that …*).
Language	1	The candidate uses a range of vocabulary, including less common lexis, appropriately (*biased, national interests, without the fear and the constant threat of an unexpected attack, entitled to a happy life*). However, there are some examples of inappropriate or inaccurate use of less common lexis (*in a tense ambiance, a great travel I did to Israel, the bellic actions, I can state with most certainty*) but there are no instances of communication being impeded.

Marks and results

Sample F (Test 4, Part 2, Question 2, Article)

Title: I was an Au pair from the Eastern Block

In today's intercultural world, one of the best assets people and nations can have is tolerance and a deep appreciation of cultural values different from their own. No wonder most training includes intercultural communication and cultural awareness courses. However, it is probably a truism that reading about or watching films about a country are only pale substitutes to actually going to visit a place and experiencing the differences yourself. And the longer you stay in a place different from what you are accustomed to, the more opportunities you have to really understand what makes people behave in a certain way, what they really like and dislike and how their community works.

For this deep experience and eventual understanding, there is no better opportunity than the year-abroad. It is an enduring tradition that has good reasons for its existence and popularity: it happens when people are in a transitional stage in their lives (usually after high school and before going to university or in between jobs), when people are relatively young and flexible in every way; physically mobile, socially unattached and adaptable, and financially not liable. However, the greatest aspect of the year abroad experience is that it can actually change your life dramatically by deciding on a course of action or career path which was not clear before.

This experience happened in my life at a time when I was (unconsciously) looking to find a value system, a community of people and – ultimately – a professional area where I wanted to make a difference for the rest of my life. I was 18, right after high school in a university town in Hungary, in 1987, wondering what to do next, when a family in England decided to invite me through a dear German friend mediating between us, to stay with them as an au pair for a year, and help out with their four children. I cannot be grateful enough for the initial offer and then the extended hospitality and life-long friendship I have with my au pair family. Most importantly, they gave me a chance at a time when my personal life as well as international politics were at a cross-roads and in a flux of change, to define a new destination and a new purpose. While the Iron Curtain was coming down, with certain unimaginable events happening one after the other – Imre Nagy's funeral, East Germans leaving their country through Hungary unchallenged by authorities, and the cathartic destruction of the Berlin Wall – my life was also going through a drastic transformation. After my year abroad experience I came back, having firmly established my identity, values and goals in life.

I would recommend the year abroad work experience to every young person who feels they need to find some guidance and self-determination in life. Apart from getting to know a culture different from your own, it helps you getting to know yourself and having the knowledge base, experience and conviction to make the next decision in life.

Subscale	Mark	Commentary
Content	5	The introduction is quite long which gives the article a slight lack of balance, but all content is relevant to the task. The target reader would be fully informed as to the experience the writer had, what made it so special and the significance of the changes in their life as a result.
Communicative Achievement	4	The candidate demonstrates a good command of the conventions of an article, communicating complex ideas in an effective and convincing way, holding the target reader's attention with ease, fulfilling all communicative purposes. The article has a suitable title and the introduction, although rather long, does succeed in engaging the target reader's interest in the topic under discussion. The recommendation at the end of the article is not strictly speaking a requirement of the task but does not significantly reduce the effectiveness of this piece of writing.
Organisation	4	The article is a well-organised, coherent whole that uses a good range of cohesive devices and organisational patterns with a very good degree of flexibility (*No wonder …, However, it is probably a truism that …, Most importantly, Apart from …*).
Language	4	A wide range of vocabulary including less common lexis, is used effectively and precisely, and often with fluency and some style (*in a transitional stage, deciding on a course of action, cathartic destruction, at a cross-roads, value system*). There are only a few instances of some slightly awkward or unnatural use of lexis (*financially not liable, eventual understanding, having the knowledge base*). The use of grammar is sophisticated, fully controlled and almost completely natural, with only a few examples of slight awkwardness or minor slips (*it helps you getting to know yourself, after my year abroad experience, I cannot be grateful enough, the greatest aspect of the year abroad experience*).

Sample G (Test 4, Part 2, Question 2, Article)

A Lonly Traveller

Whenever you think of a trip, the first thought comes to your mind is 'Who with?' If your plans are for vacations, the family is first in your mind; or your partner though I was lucky enough to have no chance to choose. It was my chief's decision to send me to London to increase my fluency in English being sure this would solve some communication problems we had in international business. When I first knew about this unexpected trip I asked 'Who with' She said 'alone'. It took me some seconds to realise it was something never realised before.

Afraid but excited I departed.

Never I had such an wonderful experience. I could plan just for myself; no other opinions considered all making decisions just of my own. If tired; I rested. If hungry I had a meal or snack, anything just for my own need. Great advantage of course the expenses just mine! I understood that depending on someone else's will or desire is the end of your own.

Being yourself is wonderful, almost imposible to describe.

This might be an experience you would never regret

You are an individual creature able to enjoy and reflect what really makes you happy and your spirit enhances just by that.

Subscale	Mark	Commentary
Content	4	All of the content is relevant to the task. The target reader would be informed as to why the travel experience was so special but the significance of resultant changes are not clearly assessed.
Communicative Achievement	0	The conventions of the article are not used with sufficient effectiveness to hold the reader's attention. A lack of logical paragraphing and the lack of grammatical accuracy in places prevent more complex ideas being successfully communicated.
Organisation	0	The text is not well organised and has no clear paragraphing. For example three paragraphs consist of single sentences and need to be part of longer paragraphs. There is very little evidence of cohesive devices being used at all, not even simple ones such as *but, in addition, finally*.
Language	0	There is a rather limited range of vocabulary (*It took me some seconds to realise it was something never realised before*) and when some range is attempted it is not always accurately used (*You are an individual creature ..., your spirit enhances just by that*). Grammatical forms are not used with much control or flexibility (*Never I had such a wonderful experience, anything just for my own need, Great advantage of course the expenses just mine*) and frequent errors can impede communication (*no other opinions considered all making decisions just of my own*).

Sample H (Test 4, Part 2, Question 5(a) (set text) Letter)

Dear Sir or Madam,

I am writing about an article that was published in your magazine's last week issue, which discussed the theme of marriage. Having recently read 'Shakespeare in Love', I now wish to express my opinion on the subject by portraying the relationships in the book.

Viola, the heroine of the story, is passionately in love with a playwright struggling with his writing. Yet, she is to marry Lord Wessex, an aristocrate who needs her in order to succeed.

The two relationships, namely between Viola and Will and between Viola and Wessex, are like night and day; or rather, like dream and reality. Indeed, the passionate love that Viola and Will share is doomed, as the two lovers do not belong in the same world. Viola is a rich lady, whereas Will, as said before, is but a poor author. Besides, Will already being married, a union is out of the question.

However, it does not mean their relationship does not succeed. It does in many different ways in fact, while Wessex, on the other hand, fails to give Viola what she needs. Indeed, Viola and Will share things that Wessex cannot even begin to understand: love, intimacy, complicity. Viola and Will complete each other: the door to inspiration opens before Will, thanks to his muse, while it is womanhood that is made available to Viola. Will flourishes as a playwright and Viola as a woman.

Viola's relationship with Wessex, by contrast, is everything but romantic. They barely know each other and there is no passion whatsoever involved. Wessex sees Viola as an object he needs to acquire. The only feeling he might have for the lady is lust. Indeed, we notice the lord's jealousy when he suspects Viola of having an affair with another man. However, he is not jealous because he loves her, but because losing her would mean losing his status, both as a lord and as a man.

To conclude, I believe that even though Viola and Will do not get their "happy ending", their relationship is the successful one.

Yours faithfully

Subscale	Mark	Commentary
Content*	4	All content is relevant to the task although the points are not developed in much detail or supported by references to the text. The target reader is on the whole informed.
Communicative Achievement	3	The conventions of the letter are used with sufficient flexibility to communicate some complex ideas, holding the target reader's attention with ease and fulfilling all communicative purposes. The format is correct with the response set out clearly as a letter, and with an appropriate introductory paragraph giving the reason for writing.
Organisation	1	The text is a well-organised and coherent and uses a variety of cohesive devices and organisational patterns to generally good effect (*indeed, whereas, as said before, in fact, on the other hand, but because, even though*). There are examples of linking words or phrases which have not been used correctly (*yet, by contrast* and the slightly awkward *To conclude*) and the word *indeed* is over-used as a way of linking ideas.
Language	3	A range of vocabulary including some less common lexis, is used appropriately (*doomed, out of the question, flourishes*). A range of simple and complex grammatical forms is used with control and some flexibility (*there is no passion whatsoever involved, both as a lord and as a man, cannot even begin to understand, is but a poor author*).

* See Briefing Document, page 152. Relevant references to the text for each set text question are listed in a Briefing Document for markers.

Marks and results

Listening

One mark is given for each correct answer. The total is weighted to give a mark out of 40 for the paper. In Part 2 spelling errors are not allowed.

For security reasons, several versions of the Listening paper are used at each administration of the examination. Before grading, the performance of the candidates in each of the versions is compared and marks adjusted to compensate for any imbalance in levels of difficulty.

Speaking

Assessment

Candidates are assessed on their own individual performance and not in relation to each other, according to the following five analytical criteria: grammatical resource, lexical resource, discourse management, pronunciation and interactive communication. These criteria are interpreted at level C2 of the CEFR. Assessment is based on performance in the whole test and is not related to particular parts of the test.

Both examiners assess the candidates. The assessor applies detailed, analytical scales, and the interlocutor applies the global achievement scale, which is based on the analytical scales.

Analytical scales

Grammatical resource

This refers to the accurate application of grammar rules and the effective arrangement of words in utterances. At level C2 of the CEFR a wide range of grammatical forms should be used appropriately and competently. Performance is viewed in terms of the overall effectiveness of the language used.

Lexical resource

This refers to the candidate's ability to use a wide and appropriate range of vocabulary to meet task requirements. At level C2 of the CEFR, the tasks require candidates to express precise meanings, attitudes and opinions and to be able to convey abstract ideas. Performance is viewed in terms of the overall effectiveness of the language used.

Discourse management

This refers to the candidate's ability to link utterances together to form coherent monologue and contributions to dialogue. The utterances should be relevant to the tasks and to preceding utterances in the discourse. The discourse produced should be at a level of complexity appropriate to level C2 of the CEFR and the utterances should be arranged logically to develop the themes or arguments required by the tasks. The extent of contributions should be appropriate, i.e. long or short as required at a particular point in the dynamic development of the discourse in order to achieve the task.

Pronunciation

This refers to the candidate's ability to produce easily comprehensible utterances to fulfil the task requirements. At level C2 of the CEFR, acceptable pronunciation should be achieved by the appropriate use of strong and weak syllables, the smooth linking of words and the effective highlighting of information-bearing words. Intonation, which includes the use of a sufficiently wide pitch range, should be used effectively to convey meaning and articulation of individual sounds should be sufficiently clear for words to be understood. Examiners put themselves in the position of the non-EFL specialist and assess the overall impact of the communication and the degree of effort required to understand the candidate.

Interactive communication

This refers to the candidate's ability to take an active part in the development of the discourse, showing sensitivity to turn taking and without undue hesitation. It requires the ability to participate competently in the range of interactive situations in the test and to develop discussions on a range of topics by initiating and responding appropriately. It also refers to the deployment of strategies to maintain and repair interaction at an appropriate level throughout the test so that the tasks can be fulfilled.

Global achievement scale

This scale refers to the candidate's overall effectiveness in dealing with the tasks in the three parts of the Cambridge English: Proficiency Speaking Test.

Marks

Marks for each scale are awarded out of five and are subsequently weighted to produce a final mark out of 40.

Test 1 Key

Reading and Use of English (1 hour 30 minutes)

Part 1
1 B   2 A   3 D   4 B   5 C   6 C   7 B   8 A

Part 2
9 up   10 come / pop   11 all   12 to   13 as   14 not   15 at
16 however

Part 3
17 likened   18 botanists   19 molecular   20 revelation
21 extraordinary   22 comparable   23 unpleasant   24 distances

Part 4
25 nothing I'd like more | than to visit/to go to
26 took (absolutely) no | notice (of me)
27 was a lack of | clarity
28 until | darkness fell
29 in the/as a last resort | does/do/will the company
30 which went into | preparing/(the)preparation (for) the OR which was taken with | preparing/(the) preparation (for) the

Part 5
31 C   32 A   33 C   34 B   35 B   36 C

Part 6
37 C   38 B   39 E   40 G   41 A   42 H   43 F

Part 7
44 E   45 C   46 A   47 B   48 D   49 B   50 A   51 C
52 C   53 F

Writing (1 hour 30 minutes)

Briefing Document

Question 1

Content
Essay must refer to and evaluate the following points:
- everybody appreciates / responds to music
- music can elicit an intense and profound emotional reaction
- music may be as important educationally as reading/writing

- all kinds of music stimulate potential
- writer's own ideas on topic.

Question 5a

Content
Article must:
- briefly describe Viola's relationships with Shakespeare and Wessex
- explain how money and position in society influence the attitudes to love of the three characters.

Answers must be supported by reference to the text. The following are possible references:
- *Viola's relationship with Shakespeare is romantic and passionate and she is his muse*
- *Viola's proposed marriage to Wessex is not based on romantic love and therefore unlikely to satisfy her emotionally: her protest to Wessex is "I do not love you, my lord." but she accepts that it is a good match*
- *Her marriage is a financial arrangement; Wessex's comment "your father has bought me for you" and Viola's lament "if they [the men at court] look at me, they see my father's fortune"*
- *Wessex has financial difficulties, whereas Viola's father has made some money from his trade and this motivates Wessex to seek an alliance with the de Lesseps. Wessex gains £5,000 from the marriage (he has a mercenary attitude).*
- *Wessex, as a nobleman, needs the permission of the Queen before marrying*
- *Daughters are expected to obey their fathers and accept the husband chosen for them; this is especially true among the upper classes*
- *Social class determines who is a suitable candidate for marriage; Viola asks Will "can a lady born to wealth and noble marriage love happily with a Bankside poet and player?"*
- *Passion is recognised as an alternative basis for love, but is not seen as a serious consideration for marriage; Will's comment, "love knows nothing of rank" and Viola's dismissal of their love affair as merely a "stolen season"*
- *Social class is seen as an insurmountable barrier to lovers from different backgrounds – NB Will's comment that "a broad river divides my lovers – family, duty, fate – as unchangeable as nature".*

Question 5b

Content
Essay must:
- explain the status of real and electric animals in the story
- evaluate their importance in society and to the characters
- refer to specific events to illustrate the points.

Answers must be supported by reference to the text. The following are possible references:
- *radioactive dust has led to the extinction of most species and all animals are protected by law*
- *owning an animal is seen as a moral and worthwhile thing to do and is a sign of empathy – they change hands for big money (Sidney's catalogue)*

Test 1 Key

- Phil Resch owns and loves a squirrel and thinks this is one reason why he can't be an android
- the belief that Mercer can bring animals back to life (e.g. spider)
- Rick's dissatisfaction at owning an electric sheep – electric animals are regarded as inferior – after seeing the 'real' owl at Rosen organisation; the organisation uses his desire to own the owl as a bribe
- seeing the ostrich gives him incentive to do his bounty hunting
- Mrs Pilsen's reaction to the death of Horace, her cat – she went to pieces
- reaction to animals used as part of Voigt-Kampff test e.g. on Luma Luft
- buying the goat as a status symbol and to establish self esteem – Iran knowing that killing it would really upset him
- Isidore's shock at the three androids' treatment of the spider – this made him upset with them
- Rick's excitement at finding what he thought was a real toad – believed to be extinct – and his disappointment when his wife shows him it wasn't
- even invertebrates are valued more highly than androids
- Rick is guilty and upset at death of a real sheep he once owned.

Listening

Part 1

1 A   2 B   3 B   4 C   5 B   6 B

Part 2

7 building / construction material   8 (world) population
9 food chain   10 microbes   11 mining   12 hormones
13 volcanoes / volcanos   14 wind   15 intensive farming

Part 3

16 B   17 C   18 A   19 D   20 C

Part 4

21 F   22 H   23 A   24 D   25 E   26 D   27 B   28 H
29 F   30 E

Transcript   Cambridge Certificate of Proficiency in English Listening Test. Test One.

I am going to give you the instructions for this test. I shall introduce each part of the test and give you time to look at the questions.

At the start of each piece, you will hear this sound:

tone

You will hear each piece twice.

Remember, while you are listening, write your answers on the question paper. You will have five minutes at the end of the test to copy your answers onto the separate answer sheet.

There will now be a pause. Please ask any questions now, because you must not speak during the test.

[pause]

Test 1 Key

PART 1 *Now open your question paper and look at Part One.*
[pause]
You will hear three different extracts. For questions 1 to 6, choose the answer (A, B or C) which fits best according to what you hear. There are two questions for each extract.

Extract 1   [pause]
tone

Man: I've just seen some statistics that show that the number of graduates taking gap years is falling steadily. That must mean that they're focusing their efforts on getting on the first rung of the career ladder as soon as possible, whatever good that does, rather than taking the chance to see something of the world before they get tied into a routine.

Woman: It's a pity, really. I know some are apprehensive about what potential bosses would think, I mean whether they'd see the gap year as a bit of a skive. It all comes down to the way it's put forward, though. If you can say what you've learnt about yourself and life, while working on, say, a community project in an inhospitable mountain valley, that cuts more ice with interviewers than lying on a beach somewhere exotic.

Man: That goes without saying. And some firms think a degree isn't enough. They'd like evidence of work-related experience, though more are realising that some of the things people get involved with in voluntary work overseas are very challenging, and may well turn them into more creative and dynamic staff members.

[pause]
tone
[The recording is repeated]

Extract 2   [pause]
tone

Most consumers go through several stages before making a purchase. First, they recognise that they have a want or a need. The consumer compares their situation to some situation they would consider to be better, and this further stimulates their want or need. In the information search stage, the person seeks information about how this want might be met. They assess past experiences; they consult external sources of information and start to weigh up the alternatives. But since humans have a limited ability to absorb information, we generally move on to the next stage knowing only some things about some alternatives.

This behaviour is of interest to marketing professionals. They look for opportunities to try to sway consumer choices toward their organisation's products. They may try to create new desires for new products, but this is costly and risky. Making sure customers aren't frustrated in making their intended purchases by offering one-click purchasing is an innovation which has proved a winner, however. We consumers are basically lazy. Few of us apparently even bother to read specifications of up-dated products before making our final decision to buy.

[pause]
tone
[The recording is repeated]

Extract 3   [pause]
tone

Interviewer: What is the single most important thing you've learned about selling online?
Man: Well, you know, there are a lot of excellent competitors around and you have to stand out to get traffic to your site. Things can change and opportunities arise with little or no notice, and being able to effectively handle the pace is what really helps or hinders a business. Actually, selling online involves many of the same concepts of traditional

127

Test 1 Key

Interviewer: retailing, using different tools and techniques. We need to remember not to get too wrapped up in the tools and techniques, but rather to clearly understand how each one supports a proven retailing concept.
Interviewer: So, what happens when it is time to grow your online business?
Man: If you've defined the next step and are attempting to grow to it, you must already have some sort of strategic plan in mind. Whatever the experts say about this being the crucial factor, you'll never get there without sufficient resources. If these aren't in place, you'll need to get creative and hit upon new backers from somewhere before moving forward.

[pause]

tone

[The recording is repeated]

[pause]

That is the end of Part One.

Now turn to Part Two.

[pause]

PART 2

You will hear a student, Hannah Jorden, giving a short talk on the topic of soil. For questions 7 to 15, complete the sentences with a word or short phrase.

You now have forty-five seconds in which to look at Part Two.

[pause]

tone

I'm going to be giving a short talk on soil. I've tried to summarise some of the main information I've found on the topic. The advantage for me is that there's a great deal of research on soil. The research often looks at one particular function that soil provides. One Canadian study I looked at focused on the importance of soil as a building material, used ever since humans first settled in communities. All studies emphasise its importance as a key to global well-being.

In today's world there's a huge amount of pressure put on how we use our soil and why we're using it. This is due to the very basic fact that the world population is rising rapidly. We need to look after our soil and natural habitats because the very survival of humankind may be at stake otherwise. And wherever we have people, we have waste. A significant amount of waste is put into landfill sites. The consequences have been serious in terms of soil pollution; once pollutants find their way into the food chain, they can damage the land and the health of any vegetation or people in the area. Dispersal of this waste through the soil also changes the composition of the soil and its ability to perform many of the functions that people and plants rely on. For example, I have seen respected data that prove that some forms of soil pollution drastically diminish the total of microbes, and this in turn decreases the biotic capability of the soil.

There are both inorganic and organic pollutants. Some of the main toxic substances are inorganic and occur as a result of mining in most continents of the world, notably the Americas, Europe and Asia. Secondary causes are smelting and the spreading of sewage on the land. In the past, it may have been ignorance or a 'couldn't care less' attitude which resulted in so much damage.

Organic pollutants often take the form of pesticides. It's now appreciated that some of the early insecticides such as DDT had a considerable impact on the environment. An area I find fascinating is the potential of organic-based pollutants to disrupt our hormones, which can have serious consequences over generations.

Many of you will know quite a bit about the effects of acid rain. This phenomenon has been with us ever since countries became industrialised and began burning fossil fuels. Then came the car, emitting its exhaust fumes into the atmosphere. However, not all the causes of acid rain are man-made; volcanoes release significant quantities of harmful gases into the atmosphere too, which then get into the soil through acid rain.

In addition to acid rain, I've also looked at soil erosion. There are two main causes of soil erosion, water and wind, and it's the latter which seems to have caught the attention of the press. It's soil erosion caused by water that's more widespread and can have more devastating effects. But soil is not only being eroded by the elements, it's also becoming weaker in terms of organic matter, which means crops aren't grown in rich soil any more. This is a result of the way we farm. As agriculturalists turn to intensive farming, this is a system which results in topsoil becoming weaker. Moreover, in recent years, because of the demand for increased crop production, cultivation has been extended more and more to sloping fields. And when it rains, a small …

[pause]

Now you will hear Part Two again.

tone

[The recording is repeated]

[pause]

That is the end of Part Two.

Now turn to Part Three.

[pause]

PART 3

You will hear part of a discussion programme, in which a teacher called Simon and a business journalist called Trina are talking about the issue of change. For questions 16 to 20, choose the answer (A, B, C or D) which fits best according to what you hear.

You now have one minute in which to look at Part Three.

[pause]

tone

Trina: If I could just come in here, Simon. I mean, there are loads of expressions in most languages to the effect that change is a good thing. In English, for example, someone who doesn't embrace change is said to be 'stuck in his ways'. If we're tired of being indoors or watching TV, we say we need a 'change of scenery', then there's a proverb which goes 'a change is as good as a rest'. So, all these are positive views of change, promoting change as something which suggests a whole host of worthy experiences to do with newness, difference, the excitement of the unknown, the adventure of the unpredictable.

Simon: True Trina, but there's also a saying, 'Don't fix it if it ain't broke'. And there's another which is 'change for change's sake'. So this is the other side of the coin, and these are expressions which represent change as something threatening, because they disturb the existing equilibrium. And I could quite easily feel both of these contrasting sentiments at different times.

Trina: What about change in the business world? I think anyone who fails to move with the times, update and adjust is doomed, because otherwise the product or service in question will no longer be relevant as time moves on. It's even a requirement of high-level jobs, specified in management contracts. It's taken as read that you have to embrace change and you're a fool if you don't. It's not even on the discussion table. The result, in practice, can be quite bewildering, with constantly shifting goals and policies and an obsession with rebranding and changing names for everything.

Simon: But in many companies it's tantamount to high treason to express a dissenting voice of conservatism, or to be seen to be putting a spanner in the works. Change is a given.

Trina: Actually, that puts me in mind of something that's evident in all walks of life, even education, and that's feedback forms. There's a bit of an obsession with being customer-led and constantly asking for customer feedback in the form of questionnaires.

Test 1 Key

Simon: Yes, you find it in libraries, museums and schools.
Trina: And it leads to a situation where the tail wags the dog. One person's sheet says, 'I didn't like x' and argues the case well, and this view is seized upon in a knee-jerk response, regardless of whether it's actually a representative comment of the larger sample, and a whole system gets changed unnecessarily.
Simon: Well, I guess if you invite people to make comments about potential changes, they'll think of anything that comes into their heads and write it, whether or not they are happy with the system that's actually in place.
Trina: Just to change the subject slightly, I was thinking that … erm … often on a day-to-day level change can be irritating: things like unexpected road works on your journey home from work. Or if you normally go swimming on a Wednesday evening at six, and then the pool times change and there's a class on instead at that time, then your routine gets broken … you had a nice little system for a while and it's really annoying until you find a way round it.
Simon: And that's typical of change. In the work environment it's initially a pain for everyone and no one likes it because they've just got confident in their new routine again following the last changes. But usually people come round to seeing the point of the change, and in due course that change becomes the new accepted status quo, which you *don't* want to change.
Trina: Yes … so does change ultimately lead to happiness?
Simon: Well … the relationship between change and perceived happiness is also interesting. There's nothing that makes me happier than going out on my bike into the countryside by myself for an hour in the sun. But I know that if I did that day in day out, I'd soon tire of it. So, I guess what I'm saying is, an activity like that is mostly enjoyable because most of the time you're stuck in an office, and so this enables you to escape from your stressful working life. If it's no longer a change, then it ceases to be something happy.
Trina: So, if you look at everything we've said …

[pause]

Now you will hear Part Three again.

tone

[The recording is repeated]

[pause]

That is the end of Part Three.

Now turn to Part Four.

[pause]

PART 4 *Part Four consists of two tasks. You will hear five short extracts in which people are talking about their involvement in award-winning projects related to the natural world. Look at Task One. For questions 21 to 25, choose from the list (A to H) what special feature of the project each speaker mentions. Now look at Task Two. For questions 26 to 30, choose from the list (A to H) what positive effect of receiving the award each speaker appreciated. While you listen you must complete both tasks. You now have forty-five seconds in which to look at Part Four.*

[pause]

tone

Speaker One: The project I received the award for was to do with a set of prehistoric animal footprints. I originally found them by chance where a storm had blown the sand off a rocky shelf by the sea, and I knew straightaway they'd been made by a species which is now extinct. I was worried the tracks would be destroyed by the fishermen who used the area, but since I've got the award, they realise how important they are. My work involved making casts of the footprints so they could be studied elsewhere, and I developed an innovative way of doing this by using silicon rubber, which produces better quality moulds than plaster.

[pause]

Test 1 Key

Speaker Two   Nowadays biologists have developed all sorts of highly specialised things to attach to animals to record their speed and heart rate and so on. But, given the enormous number of animals in need of study in the world, we need to be looking for something that can be used as a powerful, cross-species method of logging data. Although my solution is technically complex, it's so simple in concept that I call it my 'silly idea'. The award gave me the financial support I needed to develop this project further and see how it worked with different species. The data it collects will help conservationists understand habitat needs, and resolve important conservation questions.

[pause]

Speaker Three   I spend six months a year in Rajasthan, in North-West India. They used to have vast camel herds, which were used for transportation by the semi-nomadic Raika people there. But disease had decimated the herds, and undermined the livelihood of the entire community. I worked with local people to set up a training centre where we developed treatments for camels using tried and tested local herbal treatments, together with modern medicines. Receiving the award was a great acknowledgment of what we'd achieved. It also gave us the backing to get official certification of camel milk as an approved foodstuff, and the Raika people are now marketing this very cost-effective by-product.

[pause]

Speaker Four   I spent most of my life studying the whale shark. There's so much we don't know about them, and their numbers have fallen to a critical level, so I set up a project to monitor them. I had to find a way of identifying individuals, and that's what I got the award for. With the money, I've been able to recruit research assistants and show them the technique. What it's based on is, each shark has a distinctive pattern of spots on its body. So, you analyse that pattern using a technique I adapted from one that was originally used to identify star patterns, and that gives you a unique identification.

[pause]

Speaker Five   I started silkworm farming here in India 20 years ago. I used the usual techniques, but I had a lot of problems. So, I changed my approach. I'm convinced of the need to use farming methods which are environmentally benign, and I'm gradually starting to get my ideas across about what I do. That's something the award has given me the confidence to do, communicate my ideas to others. For example, I have mosquito nets to protect the silkworms, and I adapted some Japanese techniques, like, instead of traditional trays, I rear the worms in nets – they're easier to keep clean.

[pause]

Now you will hear Part Four again.

tone

[The recording is repeated]

[pause]

That is the end of Part Four.

There will now be a pause of five minutes for you to copy your answers onto the separate answer sheet. Be sure to follow the numbering of all the questions. I shall remind you when there is one minute left, so that you are sure to finish in time.

[Teacher, pause the recording here for five minutes. Remind your students when they have one minute left.]

That is the end of the test. Please stop now. Your supervisor will now collect all the question papers and answer sheets.

Test 2 Key

Reading and Use of English (1 hour 30 minutes)

Part 1

1 C   2 B   3 B   4 A   5 A   6 C   7 A   8 B

Part 2

9 mind   10 According   11 for   12 without   13 part / aspect
14 not   15 into   16 little

Part 3

17 complexities   18 misled   19 politicians   20 incredibly
21 assumptions   22 impair   23 repeatedly   24 infinite

Part 4

25 make it/mean (that) it is difficult | to reach
26 to the exhibition is restricted to | visitors/people/those who OR is restricted to the exhibition to/for visitors/people/those who
27 for Stevie's prompt action | in putting
28 is every chance/likelihood/probability/possibility | (that) taxes will rise/are (going) to rise | of taxes rising/increasing/going up
29 had/was left with no choice | but/other than to accept
30 have got into/developed/acquired | the habit of

Part 5

31 B   32 B   33 A   34 C   35 B   36 D

Part 6

37 C   38 H   39 B   40 D   41 A   42 E   43 G

Part 7

44 C   45 A   46 D   47 D   48 B   49 D   50 A   51 C
52 A   53 B

Writing (1 hour 30 minutes)

Briefing Document

Question 1

Content
Essay must refer to and evaluate the following points:
- going to the cinema is an increasingly attractive form of escapism
- films can be thought-provoking and challenge people to think about serious issues

- films are of low quality nowadays
- film studios think more about profit than originality when making films
- writer's own ideas on topic.

Question 5a

Content

Report must:
- recommend the screenplay
- briefly describe the roles of three of the following: Marlowe, the Queen, Webster, the Nurse
- assess the impact of these three characters on Will or Viola.

Answers must be supported by reference to the text. The following are possible references:

Kit Marlowe
- *regarded as the foremost playwright at The Curtain (all the actors quote from Dr Faustus in the audition); he is the talk of the town*
- *Marlowe also helps Will to get ideas for Romeo*
- *Will is jealous of Marlowe's success, but used to it*
- *Marlowe is useful scapegoat for Will when asked about Viola's lovers by Wessex*
- *when Marlowe is killed, Will feels guilty – thinks Wessex has killed him and it is his fault*
- *indirectly, death of Marlowe causes Viola to realise the depth of her true feeling for Will.*

The Queen
- *keen theatre goer and has plays written for her (she commissions Will to write a play for Twelfth Night)*
- *has approval powers over Viola as suitable wife for Wessex*
- *warns Wessex that Viola has had a lover*
- *protects Viola by saying that she is a boy dressed as a woman at end and thus makes sure theatre is not shut down.*

Webster
- *reveals nasty, brutal streak*
- *at the behest of Tilney, spies on Viola and Will making love below stage, wants to tell Wessex – unmasks Viola by throwing a mouse at her; as a result the theatre is closed down.*

Nurse
- *protects Viola, pretends that Thomas Kent is her nephew, removes theatrical moustache so that Viola's parents don't see Viola's disguise*
- *also tries to tell Viola that no good will come of what she's doing*
- *obviously loves Viola as she helps her with love affair with Will despite knowing it is wrong*
- *fulfils a maternal role for Viola.*

Test 2 Key

Question 5b

Content
Article must:
- briefly describe the future world shown in the novel
- explain what people depend on for feelings of emotional satisfaction in this future world.

Answers must be supported by reference to the text. The following are possible references:

Future world described in novel
- *population much smaller and suburbs abandoned because of radioactive dust*
- *people constantly encouraged to emigrate*
- *there are many laws governing this hierarchical society*
- *police and bounty hunters (regular humans who haven't gone to the colonies) destroy rogue androids, and bounty hunters operate in secret*
- *specials are humans who are not allowed to breed and 'drop out of history'*
- *chickenheads are specials who have failed mental facility tests*
- *androids (who are humanoid robots of countless subtypes) are becoming more and more sophisticated, especially the new Nexus 6 models, but they are hunted and killed (retired) if they have escaped from colonies and are living on Earth illegally; androids do not care about other androids.*

What people depend on for emotional satisfaction
- *people need artificial stimulation from the Penfield Mood Organ in order to help them feel a wide range of different emotions and moods. There are at least 888 settings on the Penfield Mood Organ*
- *people desperately want to own an animal and if they cannot have a real one, they will buy an electric version. Social status depends on the type of real or electric animal someone owns*
- *Rick has an electric sheep which gives him some satisfaction, but he envies his neighbour Barbour who has a real horse*
- *Rick buys a goat. Rachael says that Rick probably loves his goat more than his wife*
- *Rick is very happy when he finds what he thinks is a real toad*
- *Mercerism is a religion that gives considerable emotional satisfaction; people believe that good emotions should be transmitted and shared with others via the empathy box, a process know as "fusion"*
- *humans still get satisfaction from helping others and feeling they are not alone. Isidore feels this when he shelters the androids (whom he initially believes to be human)*
- *television provides some entertainment and escapist relief, notably the comic Buster Friendly, who is in fact an android*
- *those who emigrate have the satisfaction of owning their own android.*

Listening (approximately 40 minutes)

Part 1

1 A   2 A   3 B   4 C   5 C   6 A

Part 2

7 referees   8 injuries / injury   9 motivation   10 (academic) research
11 mental toughness   12 memory blue(-)print   13 admiration
14 insults   15 pressure / stress

Part 3

16 B   17 C   18 A   19 A   20 C

Part 4

21 G   22 C   23 F   24 H   25 B   26 H   27 G   28 B
29 F   30 D

Transcript

Cambridge Certificate of Proficiency in English Listening Test. Test Two.

I am going to give you the instructions for this test. I shall introduce each part of the test and give you time to look at the questions.

At the start of each piece, you will hear this sound:

tone

You will hear each piece twice.

Remember, while you are listening, write your answers on the question paper. You will have five minutes at the end of the test to copy your answers onto the separate answer sheet.

There will now be a pause. Please ask any questions now, because you must not speak during the test.

[pause]

PART 1   *Now open your question paper and look at Part One.*

[pause]

You will hear three different extracts. For questions 1 to 6, choose the answer (A, B or C) which fits best according to what you hear. There are two questions for each extract.

Extract 1   [pause]

tone

The received wisdom used to be that there were four tastes, and that each was perceived at a specific location on the tongue – sweet tastes at the tip, salty and then sour along the sides, and bitter at the back. This so-called 'Tongue Map' was based on some rudimentary research originally done in 1901, and then later misinterpreted. But these assumptions went unchallenged for a staggering seventy-three years, until a researcher called Virginia Collings proved that in fact every part of the tongue has receptors for every basic taste – including 'umami', a fifth taste which most Western scientists ignored until relatively recently. Why textbooks should persist in printing this so-called 'map' is quite beyond me, frankly. It certainly baffled me back when I was a

Test 2 Key

kid at school. I could never get the experiment right in science class, and I failed for insisting that I could taste sugar at the back of my mouth. Goes to show you shouldn't always take for granted what your textbook or your teachers tell you! In fact, the remarkable thing about our sense of taste is just how little is known about it.

[pause]

tone

[The recording is repeated]

Extract 2 [pause]

tone

In some ways I was fortunate to be born into a family business. When I was 14, I realised I wanted, like my parents, to work in hospitality, but also that I needed to do it in a way that felt right to me. My parents hoped I'd take over the family business as soon as possible. But I enrolled instead at a hotel management school, which led to jobs in Spain, Iran and Korea. My parents and my bosses made plenty of suggestions. I always just pretended I was listening.

But now I am chief executive of the family business. Striking the balance between respect for tradition and innovation is paramount. And I must admit I've had some real issues with the Human Resources department. To me, many HR people set too much store by a resumé, but a resumé doesn't reflect who a person is, especially in the developing world. For our business to succeed, we've got to employ people who can use their initiative. I don't want the HR department to be frightened of people like that.

[pause]

tone

[The recording is repeated]

Extract 3 [pause]

tone

Jacky: Hi, Martin. I've just been reading about power and influence as part of my course.
Martin: That sounds interesting. I've always thought that well-educated people must be able to exert power over others. Does your reading bear this out?
Jacky: You might suppose that to be true, but apparently we're all really deferential towards the ones who are introduced to us as though they were some kind of authority, you know, 'she's Head of Corporate Strategy'. It's as though we assume their views are well founded.
Martin: It's like a label which we read as 'you can trust me'. Together with the fact that they're probably earning a fortune; we're like putty in their hands.
Jacky: I was glad though to have it confirmed by research findings that gender no longer plays a part, at least not in most societies. Interestingly, the research also says that people who are seen as a lower social level aren't necessarily more easily influenced. As you'd imagine, it's more to do with self-esteem and our own feelings of worth.
Martin: Yes, I can see that.

[pause]

tone

[The recording is repeated]

[pause]

That is the end of Part One.

Now turn to Part Two.

[pause]

136

Test 2 Key

PART 2 *You will hear a sport psychologist called Brian Hawthorn giving a talk to psychology students about his profession. For questions 7 to 15, complete the sentences with a word or short phrase.*

You now have forty-five seconds in which to look at Part Two.

[pause]

tone

Hello. My name's Brian Hawthorn and I've been asked to talk to you about my chosen profession – sport psychology. Since it's a relatively new profession I'd like to give you some information about the activities sport psychologists get involved in, what techniques they employ, and why I think it's a great career.

Essentially, sport psychologists treat individual athletes and teams from complete amateurs to top professionals, as well as referees, and all of these across a raft of sporting disciplines. Our main aim is to help clients improve their performance, in particular in competitions. In order to do this we equip them with the necessary tools, by which I mean appropriate strategies, to cope with the injuries and disappointments athletes face during their sporting lives. We may also get involved in advising a coach on things like developing motivation among the players in the squad. As a sport psychologist you need good communication skills to do this.

Some sport psychologists hold full-time positions in professional sports clubs. But mostly they have a varied portfolio; for example, advising individual clients and carrying out academic research. In order to become a sport psychologist, the most likely route is via involvement in sport and a first degree in psychology, followed by accredited post-graduate training.

Now, what are the basic techniques that sport psychologists employ? There are a lot of different ones, but underlying each one of them is the aim of instilling mental toughness in competitors, as this is seen as being a crucial factor in putting in a winning performance.

Let's have a brief look at a couple of basic strategies to give you an idea of what a sport psychologist does routinely. First, let's take 'visualisation', which means preparing yourself for the challenge ahead by picturing the event in your mind. You see, through visualisation, applicants can fill in the blanks about the venue and the procedure, so they'll feel more confident and create what's known as a 'memory blueprint' of how they want to behave, for example, when answering questions which the recruitment panel may ask them.

Another technique is known as 'staying in the present'. You may well say, 'That's obvious, that's where we all are'. True, but we often have a little voice inside our head that chatters away, dwelling on past mistakes or fretting about the future, and that can interfere with what we're doing right now. For a sportsman, it can be disastrous. For instance, I worked with an international footballer who missed a penalty in the closing moments of an important match. He admitted that instead of focusing on the back of the net, he was fantasising about the admiration he would receive from his ecstatic fellow players when he scored. In other words, what he should have done was focus on the task in hand and not allow himself to get distracted by his own thoughts. It isn't only thoughts, though, that can distract. A sportsperson has to avoid being sidetracked by spectators' actions. That may be just noise in the stadium, shouting and so on, or what's becoming an increasingly common and disgraceful phenomenon, in which spectators bombard a player with insults to put him off his stride. This is just one manifestation of negative public interest. So, what marks out the real top guys? It's that they appear to 'embrace' pressure in a match or a race and actively thrive on it. And for those who don't make it to the top, it may be because they are unable to cope with this. Then once they get to the top they have to deal with …

[pause]

Test 2 Key

Now you will hear Part Two again.

tone

[The recording is repeated]

[pause]

That is the end of Part Two.

Now turn to Part Three.

[pause]

PART 3   *You will hear a programme in which Rachel and Ian White talk about their office supplies company. For questions 16 to 20, choose the answer (A, B, C or D) which fits best according to what you hear.*

You now have one minute in which to look at Part Three.

[pause]

tone

Interviewer: Rachel and Ian White started up an office supplies company eight years ago. It was hard work, but the company's now going from strength to strength. So, Rachel and Ian, what advice would you give to other people thinking of setting up their own business?

Ian: Well, one thing that was a bonus for us at first was being able to join the Brisbane Business Network. You know, it's very easy when you're running your own business to get very isolated, and so it was great being able to be around those other businesspeople, and some of them were just fantastic, the way they helped us to be more resourceful in what we were doing.

Rachel: Like when you're starting a business, I think, especially in our situation, we didn't want to think too big too fast, or spend too much money. We didn't really know what was feasible.

Ian: No, so just meeting the people and networking with them, we saw, hey, these people started out just like us and look, now they've got their own van, or they employ four people.

Rachel: Just being able to talk to them and get tips about the things that they might have stumbled on on their way to growth, you know, it's helped us so much and helped us dodge a lot of things that could've gotten in our way.

Ian: One thing we learned is, it's really important to get your website right. And it needs to be professional; so, it's worth getting someone who knows about it to design it for you. There are lots of website design companies out there.

Rachel: But they won't do all the thinking for you – you need to know what you want. We looked at the websites of some of our competitors to see how they did it. And make sure you get one that has a customer support backup. It's really important that if you have any questions you can get hold of them.

Ian: That's crucial, and it's a good idea to include information about you and who you are as a company. People have more familiarity if they actually understand a little bit more about your business – that you've won some business awards and things like that. So, all that stuff needs to be designed in.

Rachel: Then there's marketing – building up the client base and really understanding what it is that people are looking for in your product or service, what's going to pull them in.

Ian: We mostly use email marketing. Now we have a database established from people we've met, through our client base and networking, we can send out email campaigns quite efficiently without having to sit all day in the office making phone calls and things like that.

Rachel: We can just blast out messages from wherever we are – new product offers updates, and so on. In general, I think fear is a thing that holds a lot of people back, though, and it takes a lot of courage to say, 'Hey, I don't know this!' and ask for help.

Ian:	Like with the sales budget.
Rachel:	Yeah.
Ian:	We were worried about our budget. So we asked the small businesses company and they sent someone along and we had half a day looking at it. And she suggested that we should implement a budget based on our last year's figures and monitor that; and we did, and actually sales were up, and that in itself was enough to give us the power to say, hey, we're not doing too badly when you see that, regardless of whether you relate it to any other business or not.
Rachel:	We hadn't really had a precise idea of the figures before, and that gave us a tremendous amount of satisfaction.
Ian:	Yeah, that was quite a good building block for us, to establish that.
Interviewer:	So, now your company employs eight people. And I believe you now present courses on business planning?
Rachel:	Yes, we do. And what it did for me and for Ian was, by going back through those processes again, it was very enlightening for us because there were things that we hadn't actually looked at, specific aspects of the business, and we're finding that they're very valuable to pass on to those students in terms of how you set up a business plan. So, if anything, we found, if you were setting up as a new business, yes, business plans were extraordinarily valuable, but as an ongoing business they're also really good to go back to.
Interviewer:	Thank you very much and if …

[pause]

Now you will hear Part Three again.

tone

[The recording is repeated]

[pause]

That is the end of Part Three.

Now turn to Part Four.

[pause]

PART 4

Part Four consists of two tasks. You will hear five short extracts in which university students are talking about a work placement that they did. Look at Task One. For questions 21 to 25, choose from the list (A to H) how each speaker found their work placement. Now look at Task Two. For questions 26 to 30, choose from the list (A to H) what each speaker found most useful during the work placement. While you listen you must complete both tasks.

You now have forty-five seconds in which to look at Part Four.

[pause]

tone

Speaker One It wasn't easy getting a work placement. I spent ages surfing the net, researching law firms, filling in application forms, asking other law students for advice on places to try. Some firms seemed interested and then went quiet. Then it struck me a former neighbour was a solicitor in a small practice, which wasn't ideal really, but still … After some persuasion, I was offered an informal week's try-out, which was extended. It was hard getting up at 6.15 every day and working till 5.30! What made it, though, was being allowed to take over some tasks like drafting simple contracts. If I got stuck, the other staff kindly showed me what to do.

[pause]

Test 2 Key

Speaker Two	I did a work placement in a finance company. I'd heard that the best part is learning to complete work to deadlines, though I'd got that sorted handing in uni assignments. What I did every day involved using ideas I'd heard in lectures and seeing them work. That was mind-blowing and more valuable than all the stuff I had to look up for clients in the resource centre. I was very lucky, as I came across someone at a friend's wedding, who got me an interview at the company. It was a relief as I'd thought I'd have to ask my uncle, who's in banking, and I'd rather make my own way.
	[pause]
Speaker Three	I started looking for a work placement early on. I sent letters to companies I was interested in and got some positive responses. I chose one and thought it was all in hand till everything fell through. I was moaning about it to someone on my marketing course, who put me on to a car manufacturer. Not my field, so I had reservations, though needlessly as it turned out. They put me in the sales department initially. My line manager had regular sessions with me to give me pointers on how well I'd been doing and that will definitely stand me in good stead. Chatting to people during breaks was quite informative too.
	[pause]
Speaker Four	I worked in an advertising agency. It was great, though the market analysis I did was tedious. I attended meetings where senior staff presented ideas for publicising a product. Discussing those with people from the company concerned made the whole thing, really, as it showed me what avenue to follow. It would have been good to have run a project on my own, though. I got the placement in an unexpected way. I thought everything happened online, though my searches proved fruitless. I came across the agency in an advert in a marketing publication, which I replied to. The university department's so-called directory of work placements left a lot to be desired!
	[pause]
Speaker Five	I'm studying to be an accountant like my cousin, and he'd promised me a placement at his firm. He's a great guy, though up to his eyes with work, and it obviously slipped his mind. A lecturer showed me our department's database on the university server and that did the trick. I really enjoyed the placement. The staff had very different working methods, which was an eye-opener. It was demanding getting everything I'd been given done in time, though that's certainly what my work will involve. Sitting at a desk for eight hours without even getting to see any of the people whose accounts I was doing was debatable, though.
	[pause]
	Now you will hear Part Four again.
	tone
	[The recording is repeated]
	[pause]
	That is the end of Part Four.
	There will now be a pause of five minutes for you to copy your answers onto the separate answer sheet. Be sure to follow the numbering of all the questions. I shall remind you when there is one minute left, so that you are sure to finish in time.
	[Teacher, pause the recording here for five minutes. Remind your students when they have one minute left.]
	That is the end of the test. Please stop now. Your supervisor will now collect all the question papers and answer sheets.

Test 3 Key

Reading and Use of English (1 hour 30 minutes)

Part 1
1 B 2 D 3 C 4 A 5 B 6 B 7 A 8 D

Part 2
9 if 10 so 11 where 12 with / by 13 or 14 nothing 15 back 16 in

Part 3
17 environmentally 18 recycling 19 undrinkable 20 consequences
21 expectancy 22 diagnosis 23 certainty 24 speculative

Part 4
25 yourself | be taken in by 26 waited for Sophie | to finish her homework before
27 (very) last thing (that) I (would) want | is for 28 to have sustained | losses of/a loss of 29 would have been better | if I had OR | to have
30 kept in | touch/contact (regularly) with

Part 5
31 C 32 A 33 D 34 A 35 B 36 C

Part 6
37 B 38 G 39 E 40 D 41 H 42 F 43 A

Part 7
44 C 45 B 46 C 47 D 48 A 49 B 50 D 51 D
52 A 53 C

Writing (1 hour 30 minutes)

Briefing Document

Question 1

Content
Essay must refer to and evaluate the following points:
- meals shared with others provide a sense of belonging
- culinary traditions provide a sense of cultural identity
- reliance on convenience foods denies people the pleasure of cooking/eating fresh food
- preparing home-made food is a measure of hospitality
- writer's own ideas on topic.

Test 3 Key

Question 5a

Content
Review must:
- describe how characters mislead and misunderstand one another
- explain why these characters mislead one another
- consider whether their behaviour has any serious consequences.

Answers must be supported by reference to the text. The following are possible references:
- *Will talks to Viola about his love for her, thinking she is Thomas Kent, a young aspiring actor – possible consequence: start of their affair*
- *Will poses as Viola's chaperone, 'Miss Wilhelmina'; Wessex confides in 'her' and is led to believe Viola's lover is Marlowe – possible consequence: enables Will to go to court to see Wessex humiliated by the Queen*
- *Will claims to be Christopher Marlowe when challenged at Viola's house by an enraged Wessex – possible consequence: he believes he is responsible for Marlowe's death*
- *Will does not tell Viola he is married – possible consequence: she is shocked to discover it later*
- *Viola's mistaken belief that Will is dead – possible consequence: she confesses her love for him*
- *Viola pretends to be pious to delay having to see Wessex – possible consequence: Wessex is infuriated*
- *Wessex is unaware that Viola and Will are having an affair and only realises it when the Queen points it out*
- *Fennyman puts Henslowe under pressure to provide a new play – possible consequence: Will lies about progress*
- ALLOW *references to* Romeo and Juliet *when discussing misunderstandings*
- *candidates may conclude that the lies told to each other by Viola and Will don't matter in the end because they cannot be together due to the social gulf between them, as both characters admit to each other.*

Question 5b

Content
Essay must:
- briefly describe the characters of Deckard and Resch and the work that they do
- assess the extent to which their attitudes to their job change in the course of the novel.

Answers must be supported by reference to the text. The following are possible references:

Character of Rick Deckard
- *enjoys responsibility and power when testing androids with the Voigt-Kampff Empathy Test (he can even force the Rosen Corporation to abandon manufacture of their Nexus VI androids)*
- *thoughtful and conscientious; aware of the fact that a few humans may fail the Empathy Test*
- *highly motivated to work hard, so can afford to buy a real animal as an electronic one is not enough to satisfy him*

- *independent and therefore not happy to accept help from android Rachael Rosen*
- *has experienced attractions to female androids in the past and admires their talents, e.g. fine voice of android opera singer Luba Luft; has sex with android Rachael and says he would marry her*
- *takes great pride in ability to do job well, e.g. is proud of having 'retired' Polokov and of being greatest bounty hunter ever (six androids retired in 24 hours)*
- *cool and calm when under intense pressure, e.g. when Garland reveals himself to be an android*
- *highly competitive – argues with Resch over who has the right to claim the bounty for killing Luba and Garland.*

Character of Phil Resch
- *claims to be astute; able to see that Polokov was an android because of coldness and detachment*
- *highly skilled marksman and good at job*
- *owns an animal*
- *actively considers possibility that he may be an android and is shocked that he did not realise he was working for androids for a time*
- *ruthless and merciless; kills Luba Luft without any warning, mainly because she has irritated him*
- *cannot understand Rick's attitudes and doubts about his job and why Rick dislikes him*
- *sees androids as murderous illegal aliens masquerading as humans*
- *cynical; aware of problem of sexual attraction to androids, but claims bounty hunters must be more detached and sleep with them before killing them*
- *thinks love is another name for sex.*

The work of the bounty hunter
- *some rivalry between bounty hunters; Rick is annoyed when he finds that his colleague Dave Holden gets more challenging or interesting jobs*
- *bounty hunters live in fear of being shot themselves and are aware that one error could be fatal; Rick is surprised by Polokov posing as a Soviet cop*
- *financially dependent on bounty they get, rather than salary*
- *carry a weapon at all times*
- *use technology, such as the Voigt-Kampff Empathy Test, to do their job efficiently*
- *bounty hunters must follow instructions of commanding officer, even if they disagree with them*
- *other bounty hunters may have had sex with Rachael in the past, but have then been unable to kill her*
- *bounty hunters must do job unobtrusively, so that humans are not upset and do not realise that androids are around.*

How attitudes to their job change
- *initially, Rick believes androids totally incapable of empathy and that an android is not much more sophisticated than an electronic animal*
- *he believes that Mercerism gives him justification to kill androids*
- *yet even in the past, his conscience troubled him when doing his job; has been disillusioned for some time and has thought of emigrating*
- *shocked by brutal and unexpected manner in which Resch retires Luba, which makes him realise he is very different; later, he is shocked to discover that Resch is, in fact, human*

Test 3 Key

- *Rick realises for the first time that feeling empathy for androids is important and could be tested for*
- *after meeting Resch and seeing him kill Luba Luft, for the first time in his life Rick doubts his ability to do his job well*
- *his contact with Resch upsets him so much that he is only able to carry on doing his job by buying a goat*
- *feels he needs help of Rachael Rosen – help he had initially rejected*
- *after sleeping with android Rachael Rosen, considers giving up job for good); later reflects on destructive nature of what he does for a living*
- *yet in some ways, he still does not respect androids, saying they are stupid and lack emotional awareness*
- *at the end of the novel, Rick feels that he has become a different person – everything he has done in the past is now alien and unnatural to him*
- *Rick finds some sort of peace in the attitude that it is impossible to avoid doing morally wrong things and that Mercer himself had urged him to kill the androids.*

Listening (40 minutes approximately)

Part 1

1 A   2 B   3 A   4 B   5 B   6 A

Part 2

7 harbour / harbor / port   8 priests   9 frame / framework   10 puzzle
11 rope(s)   12 France   13 model   14 (bees)wax / wax from bees
15 truck / lorry

Part 3

16 D   17 C   18 A   19 D   20 C

Part 4

21 B   22 E   23 A   24 F   25 G   26 D   27 C   28 B
29 H   30 E

Transcript Cambridge Certificate of Proficiency in English Listening Test. Test Three.

I am going to give you the instructions for this test. I shall introduce each part of the test and give you time to look at the questions.
At the start of each piece, you will hear this sound:

tone

You will hear each piece twice. Remember, while you are listening, write your answers on the question paper. You will have five minutes at the end of the test to copy your answers onto the separate answer sheet.

There will now be a pause. Please ask any questions now, because you must not speak during the test.

[pause]

PART 2   *Now open your question paper and look at Part One.*

[pause]

You will hear three different extracts. For questions 1 to 6, choose the answer (A, B or C) which fits best according to what you hear. There are two questions for each extract.

Extract 1   [pause]

tone

Between 1871 and 1885, Marianne North travelled the world painting exotic, and sometimes as yet unknown, flowers, plants and trees. She recorded them with precise botanical accuracy, meticulous attention to detail, and fabulous colours. Her subjects are all set in their own environment, some in a jungle, others on the side of a mountain, looking across a valley, or amongst other foliage. This collection of paintings depicts landscapes across the globe, and it is an invaluable record of a world untainted by mass tourism and commercialisation.

   Marianne North was a remarkable person for her time. As a nineteenth-century female of the middle classes, she'd have had limited schooling. But being able to draw and paint was an essential accomplishment for a young lady of her social standing. Nowadays, it's seen as just one of those things we may, or may not, take to a bit at school, isn't it? But Marianne would have been encouraged from an early age. Obviously she had talent, but it was not until she started travelling, at the age of forty, that it really, you could say, blossomed.

[pause]

tone

[The recording is repeated.]

Extract 2   [pause]

tone

Interviewer: Professor Renton, what initially attracted you to science?
Professor: Well, in fact it was my fascination with the fictional detective Sherlock Holmes: the way he uses first-hand evidence and analytical reasoning to solve his mysteries. My father and grandfather were both engineers. Engineers tend to take things apart. Although they're not always able to reassemble them, they're always curious about how things work. That's doubtless in my genes, too. In Sherlock Holmes stories you're offered the pieces of the jigsaw, and he puts it all together. Readers are always thrilled by the moment when it all comes clear – and you get lots of those in science.
Interviewer: I believe you have plans for changing the museum's image.
Professor: Yes, indeed. The perception is that it looks backwards through its collection – that it's historical. I'd like it to be sufficiently up-to-date that someone watching a TV programme expressing doubts about climate change might think, 'I'm confused about climate change. I'd better go to the Science Museum and see what they're presenting so I can make up my mind.' Basically, I want it to be seen as 'the museum of the future'.

[pause]

tone

[The recording is repeated.]

Extract 3   [pause]

tone

Of course, the Internet's great – I can do an internet search and find the exact location of this restaurant on the edge of Liverpool, or whatever. But the people whose working patterns have been significantly changed by the Internet are in a tiny minority. When

145

Test 3 Key

you look at its impact on the economy, it's mainly in the area of leisure. For most people, its effect is more about keeping in touch with friends and looking up things here and there, although there's now so much information out there that you don't actually have time to digest it.

In fact, I believe the washing machine was more transformative. By liberating women from household work and helping to abolish professions such as domestic service, the washing machine completely revolutionised the structure of western society. And this had huge economic consequences. Rather than spend their time washing clothes, women could go out and do more productive things, so it doubled the workforce. Of course, it's not just the washing machine; it's piped water, it's electricity, it's irons and so on. But the feminist movement couldn't have been implemented without this technological basis.

[pause]

tone

[The recording is repeated.]

[pause]

That is the end of Part One.

Now turn to Part Two.

[pause]

PART 2

You will hear part of a lecture about ancient Egyptian ships and an attempt to reconstruct one. For questions 7 to 15, complete the sentences with a word or short phrase.

You now have forty-five seconds in which to look at Part Two.

[pause]

tone

We know that the ancient Egyptians built ships, but until recently people thought these were just for river transport. For example, the remains of an elegant wooden ship 4,500 years old were found by the Great Pyramid, but this wouldn't have been strong enough to go out to sea.

However, archaeologists working at the desert site of Mersa Gawasis, on the shores of the Red Sea, about 160 km from the famous temples of Luxor, have recently started uncovering amazing artefacts – things like stone anchors and planks of wood that were once part of ships – and they now believe this was the site of a harbour from where ships sailed down the Red Sea.

They believe the ships were sent out by Hatshepsut, a woman who ruled over Egypt 3,500 years ago. She already had a strong army, but, to retain her power as pharaoh, she had to have the backing of the priests, and one way of getting this was to provide them with the incense they burned during religious ceremonies. This wasn't available in Egypt, so she had it brought in by ship. Support for this theory comes from carvings made at the time, of sailing ships, with their crew, sails and cargo all shown in amazing detail.

So, a team attempted to reconstruct one of these ships to find out whether it actually could carry out a sea voyage. They started by examining both the remains of the river ship and the carvings of Hatshepsut's ships to find out as much as they could about the design of ships. They were surprised to find that, while modern shipbuilders start by constructing a framework and then build the ship round it, the ancient Egyptian shipbuilders didn't do this – instead the planks of wood which formed the outside of the ship were carefully shaped so that they all fitted together. Constructing the whole thing out of so many differently-shaped pieces of wood must have been rather like trying to solve a puzzle, but on a huge scale, and without knowing if there was actually a solution or not.

146

Test 3 Key

This was true for both the river ships and for seagoing ships, but in other ways there were differences in their construction. For example, the pieces of wood on the river ship had holes in at regular intervals, not for nails as in modern ships, but for ropes, to add more support, and keep the planks from coming apart. But there was no evidence of this on the carvings of the seagoing ships. Instead, they relied solely on wooden joints.

Reconstruction of the ship required massive pieces of wood. Egypt has never been a great place to find giant trees, and the pharaohs used cedar trunks, imported from Lebanon. But today, the cedars of Lebanon are rare, so the timber was imported from France, from 150-year-old Douglas-fir trees.

The actual building of the ship was carried out by the Lahma family, several brothers who run a shipyard in Egypt and have a lot of experience with modern wooden ships. Rather than the archaeologists providing them with a written, two-dimensional plan, they provided the brothers with a model of what was required. No-one's built a ship like this for three thousand years, but the Lahma brothers were able to understand the way it all fitted together, and translate this to the real thing.

Once the ship was built, one problem remained. There were still cracks between the planks of wood, which would mean that it'd leak when it was floated on water. Modern wooden ships use epoxy resin, but that wasn't available 3,000 years ago, so they decided to use beeswax instead. They knew the ancient Egyptians were familiar with this and that they used it on their furniture.

So finally, the ship was ready. The inscriptions on the carvings had said that the seafaring ships were constructed on the River Nile, and that they were taken apart again, plank by plank, and carried across the desert to the Red Sea by donkey. But the research team decided to cheat a little here and, instead of dismantling the ship, they loaded the entire thing onto a truck and drove it there.

So at last, they were ready to launch the ship. But they'd no idea how it would perform ...

[pause]

Now you will hear Part Two again.

tone

[The recording is repeated.]

[pause]

That is the end of Part Two.

Now turn to Part Three.

[pause]

PART 3   *You will hear two costume design students, Angela and Mike, discussing the role of costumes in films. For questions 16 to 20, choose the answer (A, B, C or D) which fits best according to what you hear.*

You now have one minute in which to look at Part Three.

[pause]

tone

Angela: I'm really enjoying this course, aren't you, Mike?
Mike: Yes, it really makes you sit up and think; there's never a dull moment.
Angela: Right from the start I was riveted; do you remember one of the first things we had to do was watch a film without any sound? That in itself isn't anything new, I know; it's done on lots of courses, like script writing, to see if you can get the storyline just from visual input, like what people are wearing, but to ask us to watch like that and then halfway through be asked to say who would befriend who, and who would fall out with who was great!

147

Mike:	Yes, you could easily see if the characters were angry, etc. from their facial expression, but the questions made us look closely at costume to see what else might be revealed about them. And it's amazing to think that even the main ideas of the film can be conveyed partially through costume when a good costume designer's been at work.
Angela:	Yes. I'm loving all the modules on this course. I did history, art and design and media studies at school and this course incorporates all of those subjects, and more.
Mike:	Yes, and academic topics such as the role of film as documentation of social history and how businesses look to film for fashion ideas are offset with practical modules like pattern cutting and sewing, which I'm drawn to in particular.
Angela:	And even where to go, flea markets, museums and costume warehouses and so on, to try to find exactly the right handbag or umbrella for a particular scene.
Mike:	Sounds good if you've got the time, I suppose. I really enjoyed that last session when we watched a film and then the whole group discussed the costumes. We talked about a female character who wore layers and layers of clothes, and we were asked what that signified about her character. I thought people's suggestions that it made her seem secretive or that it suggested there were many 'layers' to her personality seemed perfectly reasonable.
Angela:	I know, but when someone said it meant she was timid, it didn't go with the way she was in the film.
Mike:	And they were layers of brightly-coloured, rather flamboyant clothes, so hardly!
Angela:	It's an important point, though, that clothes are a part of our identity.
Mike:	The thing is, as a costume designer working for a film studio, you can't always do exactly what you want. You have to make compromises. The director may tell you to make a costume in a certain way because he needs it like that because of the lighting or something.
Angela:	Or that the actor's going to be in a fight scene, so he needs to be able to jump and run easily. I think the problem with working on a film as opposed to being students, like we are now, is you'd have to get the costumes ready for filming within a couple of months and you wouldn't have time to find out everything you needed to know before you started work on them.
Mike:	Absolutely, and do you think money plays a part? You can't spend a fortune on every costume.
Angela:	That must vary from studio to studio.
Mike:	Right. Have you decided what to do your next project on? I bet you're doing something on female actors and how clothes show how women's role in society has changed.
Angela:	More how certain things like trousers were first seen as part of women's liberation but a couple of decades later were seen as merely utilitarian. I'd thought about looking into project managing the manufacture of huge numbers of costumes for crowd scenes and things like that, but it seems to involve a lot of finance and figures, and that put me off.
Mike:	Yes, and I think looking just at the lead character in any film may not have enough scope for the sort of project we've got to submit.
Angela:	Right.

[pause]

Now you will hear Part Three again.

tone

[The recording is repeated.]

[pause]

That is the end of Part Three.

Now turn to Part Four.

[pause]

Test 3 Key

PART 4 *Part Four consists of two tasks. You will hear five short extracts in which people are talking about their experiences in their first jobs. Look at Task One. For questions 21 to 25, choose from the list (A to H) what skill each speaker developed during their first job. Now look at Task Two. For questions 26 to 30, choose from the list (A to H) what each speaker appreciated most in their first job. While you listen, you must complete both tasks.*

You now have forty-five seconds in which to look at Part Four.

[pause]

tone

Speaker One   My first job taught me a lot, particularly in terms of what I can get done in a short period. I learnt to juggle and multi-task like never before. The early starts were the worst, so in the end I moved into the hotel – this was great, as I was offered any overtime first. The best thing was the on-the-job experience and learning from the old guys; they got me doing things instead of just talking about them. If I hadn't had to return to Uni, I would probably have stayed on and, who knows, I could have been the manager by now.

[pause]

Speaker Two   I worked in an office with about 20 other people and we all got on, but very superficially. I found it difficult because I was one of the youngest, but had to conduct appraisals, trying to find the right words. It was a really busy environment, no time to build friendships. One day, the boss decided to introduce a programme of social events, starting with a team-building weekend. This was the first time we had spent any time together away from work and we were all a bit sceptical, but it was amazing. I felt I had more confidence in conducting evaluations, and my colleagues accepted my comments objectively.

[pause]

Speaker Three   After I finished my degree in the UK, I couldn't find any suitable well-paid jobs. I figured if I was going to work for a pittance, I might as well do something useful. I volunteered and went to a village in Kenya. There were no set working patterns, which suited me as I preferred to work until the job was done and then relax, chatting to the villagers. I picked up the language after about six months and this came in useful when an English businessman came to present his ideas for new sports facilities for the village. I managed to negotiate between both sides to set up a football training centre for the village.

[pause]

Speaker Four   When looking for my first job, I didn't really know what I was good at, but I think I fell on my feet. I took a job as a tourist information officer in a different country, getting by on rudimentary language skills. Initially, I was used on the front desk because of my English, but I was soon moved to an admin position in the back when I found that I had a talent for spreadsheets and extrapolating meanings from numbers. When the position of assistant manager came up, I was encouraged to go for it, so I did. I've never looked back, and friends from home love coming over here to visit.

[pause]

Speaker Five   After an argument with my first boss, I told him that I was leaving to set up my own company. I was amazed when he suggested I should stay and offered me a different position, where I would be able to make changes. He'd recognised that I was frustrated

Test 3 Key

in my position and that I had a vision which he felt could be useful. I realised leaving wouldn't fix anything, and that I actually wanted to learn how to sort out the issues affecting workforces. He was giving me an opportunity to troubleshoot, and I relished it. It wasn't a higher-level position, but, actually, I appreciated the opportunity he'd given me.

[pause]

Now you will hear Part Four again.

tone

[The recording is repeated.]

[pause]

That is the end of Part Four.

There will now be a pause of five minutes for you to copy your answers onto the separate answer sheet. Be sure to follow the numbering of all the questions. I shall remind you when there is one minute left, so that you are sure to finish in time.

[Teacher, pause the recording here for five minutes. Remind your students when they have one minute left.]

That is the end of the test. Please stop now. Your supervisor will now collect all the question papers and answer sheets.

Test 4 Key

Reading and Use of English (1 hour 30 minutes)

Part 1
1 C   2 B   3 A   4 B   5 C   6 D   7 A   8 B

Part 2
9 for   10 back   11 degree / extent   12 given   13 anything
14 little   15 in   16 danger

Part 3
17 virtuous   18 downside   19 sleepless   20 insignificance
21 necessarily   22 emissions   23 Additionally   24 disastrous

Part 4
25 (that) there is no change/there are no changes | to/in Sam's plans
26 no reason to suppose (that) | Simon will not OR every reason to suppose (that) | Simon will   27 was there (any/an) official | acknowledg(e)ment of/as to/regarding   28 no account | are passengers (allowed/permitted)   29 am at a (complete) loss | to understand/to know/as to   30 has no intention | of making

Part 5
31 C   32 B   33 A   34 C   35 D   36 A

Part 6
37 D   38 G   39 A   40 H   41 E   42 B   43 F

Part 7
44 C   45 B   46 A   47 C   48 B   49 D   50 B
51 D   52 A   53 C

Writing (1 hour 30 minutes)

Briefing Document

Question 1

Content
Essay must refer to and evaluate the following points:
- it's possible to lose the enjoyment of reading if you have to do too much of it
- choice of a book as a child says something about personality / future career
- reading aloud is an enriching experience for all ages
- sharing the experience of listening to something read aloud increases enjoyment
- writer's own ideas on topic.

Test 4 Key

Question 5a

Content
Letter must:
- compare Viola's relationships with Wessex and Will
- explain why Viola marries Wessex and not Will.

Answers must be supported by reference to the text. The following are possible references:

Arranged marriage with Wessex
- *marriage arranged without consulting Viola and she does not love him*
- *financially advantageous to Wessex and important to Viola's father because of Wessex's name and position in society*
- *Wessex wants a wife to be 'obedient and fertile'*
- *Wessex can arrange this marriage because of his position in society, has the Queen's approval*
- *Viola must accept the marriage because of her sex and position in society ('I will do my duty').*

Relationship between Will and Viola
- *Viola is infatuated with Will as a writer rather than a man at first*
- *romantic passion between Will and Viola ('like a riot in the heart')*
- *Viola can see the reality that their relationship cannot last ('a stolen season')*
- *there is some dishonesty in their relationship; Will is already married*
- *they cannot marry because of the difference in social status (Will: 'love knows nothing of rank'; Viola takes a more realistic attitude).*

Question 5b

Content
Review must:
- briefly explain the themes of love and loneliness with reference to the characters Deckard and Isidore
- assess whether it is the treatment of the themes of love and loneliness that make the book worth reading.

Answers must be supported by reference to the text. The following are possible references:

Rick Deckard
- *Rick Deckard feels a degree of attraction and affection for androids; he is fond of Luba Luft and buys her a print*
- *he is attracted to Rachael Rosen and sleeps with her, and feels that he wants to marry her; Phil Resch, in contrast, has no qualms about sleeping with an android and then killing her*
- *Rick loves his goat more than his wife*
- *Rick can only connect emotionally or sexually with his wife via the Penfield Mood Organ*

- *all humans feel lonely, but with the empathy box can experience feelings of 'fusion' with other humans; however, when Rick's wife uses the box he feels lonely*
- *when Rick buys a goat, Iran urges him to share his feelings of happiness with everyone else via the empathy box.*

John Isidore
- *Isidore feels alone in his apartment block and is delighted when Pris appears in his apartment*
- *he is happy to protect the three androids Pris, Irmgard and Roy Baty, and to feel he has some purpose in life; he feels sorry for them and is told that androids feel lonely too*
- *he believes that 'you have to be with people to live at all well'*
- *television provides an escape from loneliness for Isidore in his empty apartment block*
- *Isidore is isolated from others because his apartment is unoccupied, with only the empathy box to connect him to others, and he is treated with contempt by his employer, Hannibal Sloat.*

Listening (40 minutes approximately)

Part 1
1 B   2 A   3 C   4 B   5 B   6 A

Part 2
7 white leopard   8 living fossil   9 thumb   10 grass(es)   11 mood
12 barking   13 mountain(ous)   14 green corridors   15 vulnerable

Part 3
16 B   17 D   18 C   19 B   20 A

Part 4
21 F   22 H   23 B   24 E   25 G   26 F   27 E   28 H
29 B   30 A

Transcript *Cambridge Certificate of Proficiency in English Listening Test. Test Four.*

I am going to give you the instructions for this test. I shall introduce each part of the test and give you time to look at the questions. At the start of each piece, you will hear this sound:

tone

You will hear each piece twice. Remember, while you are listening, write your answers on the question paper. You will have five minutes at the end of the test to copy your answers onto the separate answer sheet.

There will now be a pause. Please ask any questions now, because you must not speak during the test.

[pause]

Test 4 Key

PART 1   *Now open your question paper and look at Part One.*

[pause]

You will hear three different extracts. For questions 1 to 6, choose the answer (A, B or C) which fits best according to what you hear. There are two questions for each extract.

Extract 1   [pause]

tone

Interviewer: Sarah, what is Online Now?
Sarah: Basically, we want to achieve a networked nation. So, Online Now is a campaign to get at least 95% of the population online in the next two years.
Interviewer: Why such a rush?
Sarah: We have to rush because we're just being flooded with data. Every single day, for example, the government's saying: 'Comment on our budgets' – important things that are going to affect communities deeply. At the end of most advertising, it's 'Get a special deal online'. So we can't wait, because society is splintering as we speak. I don't want to live in a community where a huge number of people are being excluded from the conversation that everyone else is having.
Interviewer: But if everyone's going to be online, where will the equipment come from?
Sarah: We're not advocating that everyone has a computer at home. There'll always be people for whom this is too expensive. We have to be pragmatic about what we can do. There's been so much IT investment into communities – into schools, into health centres, into libraries. I would like the government to consider better ways of exploiting those bits of technology.

[pause]

tone

[The recording is repeated.]

Extract 2   [pause]

tone

This stone pestle comes from Papua New Guinea. It stands about 35 cm tall, and the business end is a stone bulb, about the size of a cricket ball, and you can feel that it's been used a lot. Above the bulb, the handle is very easy to grasp and its upper part's been shaped in a way that's got nothing to do with making food – it looks like a bird with outstretched wings and a long neck dipping forward. We think it's about eight thousand years old.

So, we know that at that time farmers in Papua New Guinea grew a starchy tuber called taro, while in the Middle East, they were cultivating grasses, types of wheat, and in China, rice. But what's interesting is that in their natural state you can't eat any of these plants; you have to grind them or soak them or boil them first. So, why choose them? Well, the answer is that as humans expanded across the globe, we had to compete for our food with other animals. So, we went for food that was difficult, and that gave us a competitive advantage.

[pause]

tone

[The recording is repeated.]

Extract 3   [pause]

tone

The health of our oceans is in decline and yet, there seems to be little attempt by governments or businesses to intervene. Global warming is one issue, increasing the acidity of the sea water to the detriment of marine life, but, more seriously, despite regulations to stop overfishing and opportunistic fishermen landing illegal catches to sell on the black market, international laws seem to be interpreted at a local level. One conservation solution is to introduce more marine reserves similar to one in the Pacific Ocean, where commercial fishing is banned and regular checks are carried out on all aspects of marine wildlife.

Conservation projects focusing on single high-profile species, such as sharks and sea birds like the albatross, frequently draw attention away from the more serious damage being done to food sources like algae, which leads to the death of many more species. One proposal is to gather data from all the oceans and produce an ocean health index, which would then be published globally. From this, governments and businesses would be able to see instantly how their actions are affecting the health of the oceans close to them.

[pause]

tone

[The recording is repeated.]

[pause]

That is the end of Part One.

Now turn to Part Two.

[pause]

PART 2

You will hear a talk about a Chinese animal called the giant panda. For questions 7 to 15, complete the sentences with a word or short phrase.

You now have forty-five seconds in which to look at Part Two.

[pause]

tone

I'd like to tell you about the giant panda, which is a bear that's native to China, and one of the world's best-loved and most easily recognised animals.

The giant panda is a national emblem of China, and over history the Chinese have given it over twenty different names. Among them are names translating as 'spotted bear' – describing its black and white body, 'bamboo bear' – referring to its diet and, rather strangely, 'white leopard', possibly because of its tree-climbing abilities. Then there's the current, most frequently used term, 'cat bear', which is also echoed in the scientific Latin name for the species.

There's been much debate about how to classify the giant panda, although recent molecular studies seem to confirm that it is actually a bear. However, the species differentiated early in history from all other bears, making it the only member of an otherwise extinct branch of the family. For that reason, it is considered by certain experts to be a living fossil. The animal known as the red panda, which shares its habitat, is in fact only a very distant relative.

Although the giant panda is classed as a carnivore, its sustenance comes almost exclusively from the bamboo plant. With its large molar teeth and strong jaw muscles, the giant panda is ideally suited to bamboo eating. And in addition to the five fingers on each paw, it also has an elongated wrist bone, which it uses as if it were a thumb. This helps it pull up and grip tough bamboo shoots.

Because bamboo has little nutritional value, the giant panda has to consume up to 14 kilos of it per day. It eats all of the twenty-five different bamboo species native to its habitat, but will, on occasion, supplement this diet with other kinds of grasses, and even meat, in the form of various birds and rodents.

The giant panda is a solitary creature with relatively poor vision but an acute sense of smell, and so relies principally on scent to communicate with other individuals. It secretes a strong-smelling substance from its glands, which it rubs onto trees and stones on the edges of its territory. These scent markings convey an enormous amount of information, not only about the animal's gender, state of health and even their mood, but also how long ago the 'message' was left.

Test 4 Key

Unlike some other animals, the giant panda can't communicate via facial expression, or even ear or tail position. But it does produce a surprising range of vocalisations, including a honking sound to indicate distress, a barking sound to convey antagonism to enemies, and a number of chirps and bleating sounds used as friendly contact calls.

The giant panda used to live in a vast forest area, but, due to extensive farming and deforestation, much of its habitat has been destroyed, leaving only small populations in a handful of mountain areas in the country. Current estimates of numbers remaining in the wild range between only one and two thousand individuals.

Isolated populations, living in so-called 'wildlife islands', could also face eventual starvation. When the bamboo dies off, animals are unable to migrate to other areas where a different bamboo species is thriving. The key to saving these communities is schemes which plant what are termed 'green corridors' – made up of native tree species and bamboo – which link the wildlife islands, and so facilitate migration.

Thanks to projects such as these, the number of giant pandas in the wild is said to be rising. However, the International Union for Conservation of Nature doesn't believe there's enough certainty to change the giant panda's conservation status on its Red List of Threatened Animals. It's declined to downgrade its current status of Endangered to the less crucial status of Vulnerable. Even so, the future is still looking a little brighter for China's favourite black and white bear.

[pause]

Now you will hear Part Two again.

tone

[The recording is repeated.]

[pause]

That is the end of Part Two.

Now turn to Part Three.

[pause]

PART 3

You will hear part of a programme in which Amanda and Peter, two founders of a fruit juice company called Topfruit, talk about their business. For questions 16 to 20, choose the answer (A, B, C or D) which fits best according to what you hear.

You now have one minute in which to look at Part Three.

[pause]

tone

Presenter:	I'm delighted to welcome to the programme this evening Amanda Fry and Peter Davy, two of the founders of the company Topfruit, that makes delicious blends of fruit juice. What's it like setting up a company with friends?
Amanda:	Well, we've all seen friends falling out, take some of the famous rock bands, for instance. I must say though that for us it was quite the reverse. I believe trust is the most efficient thing in business terms. It means you don't need to keep checking up on people. You see, the four of us have been mates since university days and there's amazing alignment in our values and ambitions.
Peter:	Yet our skills are complementary. As a result there was no squabbling when it came to deciding who should focus on different areas, such as retailers, operations or consumers, because it was self-evident. Actually, I'm in awe of people who set up a company on their own. How they encompass all those aspects is a mystery to me.
Amanda:	But, coming back to our company, it certainly is a great place to work. We pride ourselves on having an open and co-operative culture. Whether we can take any credit for that, I'm not sure. I think it's all down to the staff. What we made a point of at the beginning, was only to select people we liked and whose values chimed with those of the business. After that, you could perhaps say it's a belief in the importance of making

	a healthy product to enhance customers' well-being. I wouldn't want you to think that it's all fun and games, though. In line with current thinking, there's a tough performance management system – everyone's assessed regularly against a number of objectives and the results are linked to pay increases.
Peter:	Personally, it took me ages to be able to arrive at work on a Monday without imagining all sorts of disasters, you know, like crowds of angry customers or a bankruptcy notice. As for how I feel about running the company now: it's still a very demanding business and it's like being on a rollercoaster with its ups and downs. That's where the buzz comes from, though.
Amanda:	Strangely, I reckon it would be boring if everything were on an even keel. You'd stop trying.
Peter:	And we all make mistakes, don't we?
Amanda:	Absolutely. As the company's grown, we've made some bad choices when recruiting senior people. We interviewed someone with a fantastic CV, an MBA and loads of relevant experience, and assumed he'd be great, but neglected to check whether he'd fit in with the ethos of the company and the existing team, and he didn't. Another one was perfect in that respect, but had never held a top post. I tried to kid myself that with good mentoring he'd get there, and so, I kept him on too long. I should've realised from the outset that he was wrong for the job. One thing was clear, though; it was our fault, not theirs.
Peter:	But we have managed to hold our own against the corporate giants who are our major competitors. There are a number of reasons why. First, the concern we express about wholesome food and getting our fruit from reliable sources strikes a chord with many consumers at the moment, so our juices tick those boxes.
Amanda:	Then our marketing's straightforward and transparent, even down to using very basic clear bottles so the juice can be seen easily on the shelf.
Peter:	And it doesn't come with the usual hype and polish, since we do it all in-house, without employing the services of an ad agency to design a trendy image.
Amanda:	Customer research is done in a similar way, too. We take samples of new blends round events like music festivals and food fairs, and get feedback that way, so people feel directly concerned.
Peter:	We're often asked …
	[pause]
	Now you will hear Part Three again.
	tone
	[The recording is repeated.]
	[pause]
	That is the end of Part Three.
	Now turn to Part Four.
	[pause]
PART 4	*Part Four consists of two tasks. You will hear five short extracts in which some sports-people are talking about their sporting successes. Look at Task One. For questions 21 to 25, choose from the list (A to H) what each speaker regards as the key to winning in sport. Now look at Task Two. For questions 26 to 30, choose from the list (A to H) what each speaker sees their coach as. While you listen, you must complete both tasks.*
	You now have forty-five seconds in which to look at Part Four.
	[pause]
	tone
Speaker One	My coach has always said to me, 'Tennis is a bit like driving – you have to think for two and be continually thinking about what's going to happen, or what shot your opponent is about to play.' I agree that, ultimately, this is what separates the champion from the also-ran. You won't catch him spouting all the psycho-babble around in the sports

Test 4 Key

community these days. He thinks the only kind of advice worth giving is the 'two hours' sleep before midnight is worth one after midnight' sort of advice that your grandmother knew! And that attitude reflects in his coaching style.

[pause]

Speaker Two We played American football at school, and our team virtually never lost. We just had some really huge guys built like brick walls, and a tough reputation, which we really lived up to – we really used to psych out our opponents. So, they would already be in a negative frame of mind before they started, ready for a bad experience and they'd play for damage limitation. Our coach was well aware of this, of course. He'd try to reinforce the idea in our heads that we were invincible, so we all regarded him as someone who gave us our winning edge.

[pause]

Speaker Three There's a new idea about putting the athlete at the heart of the training process, and my coach and I very much subscribe to this. His role is to empower me to take responsibility for my development. My motivation is entirely internal – for instance, I read this book called *How to produce champions* recently. It really struck a chord with me. Basically, the author was trying to debunk the myth that being a champion is all in your genes. And his point was that a few years ago, six of the top ten British gymnasts practised at the same gym – they pushed each other on to greater things.

[pause]

Speaker Four My coach has drummed into me that it's all about having no single drop of doubt in your brain about the great talent you were born with. For me, that's taken as read – any serious competitor thinks that. So I'd go beyond that, I'd say it's about leaving no stone unturned – the diet must be perfect; the training must leave nothing out. And, you know, in my case I can take my lead from my coach in this respect, because he takes the view that he can't demand from you what he doesn't show himself. Both of us are always full of ideas for training, so we can bounce them off each other.

[pause]

Speaker Five With my team two years ago, there was a kind of force that drove us and bound us together – we'd do anything for each other. But right at the end of the season injuries struck and we ended up having to settle for second place. Last year we were on a losing streak until injuries hit our top rivals. And after that, fortune continued to favour us and we just kept on winning matches that we had no right to win. Our coach also helped. I'll never forget the game where he took off two defenders and brought on two attackers. It was a potentially disastrous strategy, but, as always, it worked!

[pause]

Now you will hear Part Four again.

tone

[The recording is repeated.]

[pause]

That is the end of Part Four.
There will now be a pause of five minutes for you to copy your answers onto the separate answer sheet. Be sure to follow the numbering of all the questions. I shall remind you when there is one minute left, so that you are sure to finish in time.
[Teacher, pause the recording here for five minutes. Remind your students when they have one minute left.]
That is the end of the test. Please stop now. Your supervisor will now collect all the question papers and answer sheets.

Sample answer sheet: Reading and Use of English

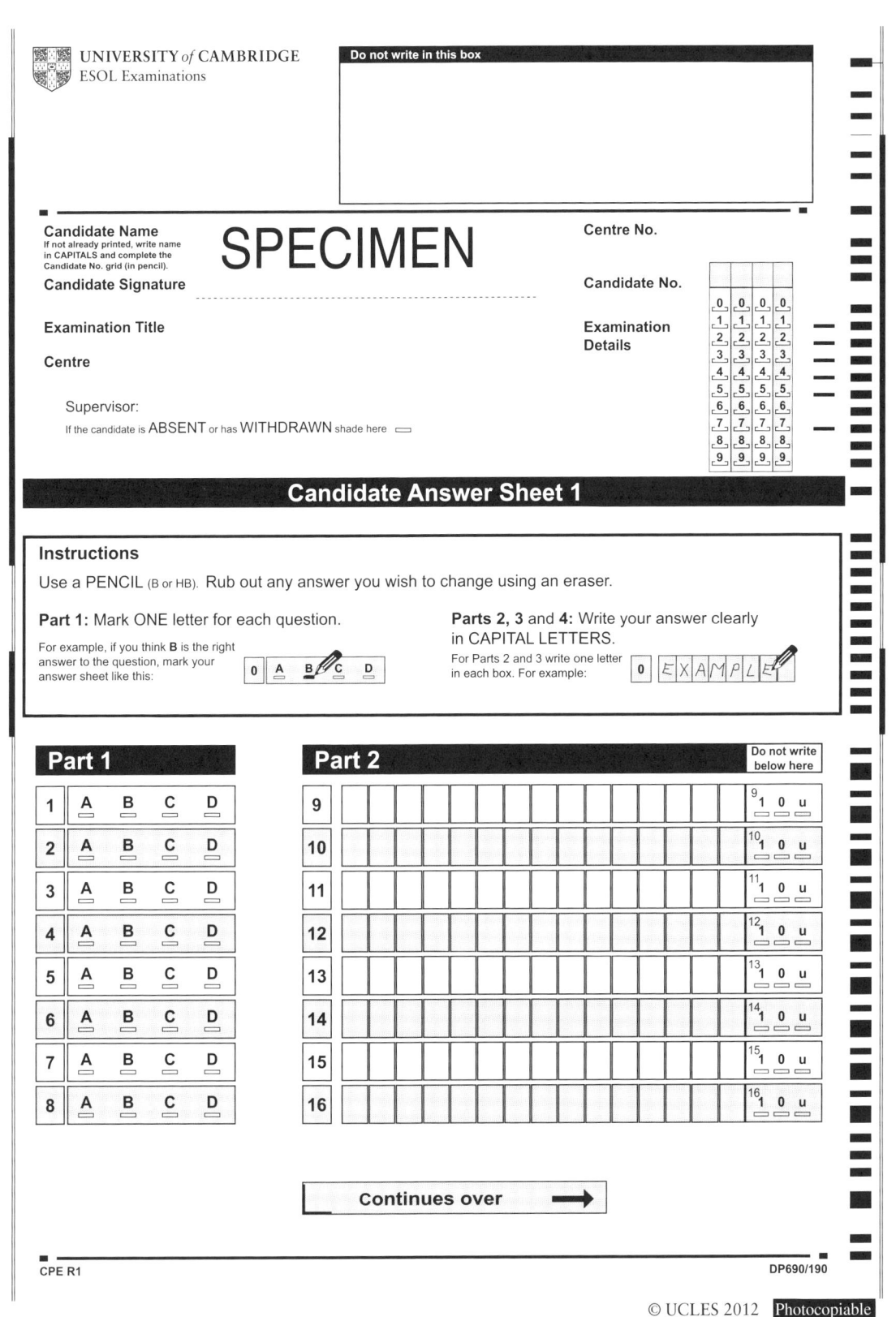

UNIVERSITY of CAMBRIDGE
ESOL Examinations

Do not write in this box

Candidate Name
If not already printed, write name in CAPITALS and complete the Candidate No. grid (in pencil).

Candidate Signature

SPECIMEN

Examination Title

Centre

Supervisor:
If the candidate is ABSENT or has WITHDRAWN shade here ▭

Centre No.

Candidate No.

Examination Details

Candidate Answer Sheet 1

Instructions

Use a PENCIL (B or HB). Rub out any answer you wish to change using an eraser.

Part 1: Mark ONE letter for each question.

For example, if you think **B** is the right answer to the question, mark your answer sheet like this: `0  A  B̸  C  D`

Parts 2, 3 and **4:** Write your answer clearly in CAPITAL LETTERS.

For Parts 2 and 3 write one letter in each box. For example: `0 | E | X | A | M | P | L | E`

Part 1

1	A B C D
2	A B C D
3	A B C D
4	A B C D
5	A B C D
6	A B C D
7	A B C D
8	A B C D

Part 2

9, 10, 11, 12, 13, 14, 15, 16

Continues over ➡

CPE R1

DP690/190

© UCLES 2012 Photocopiable

159

Sample answer sheet: Reading and Use of English

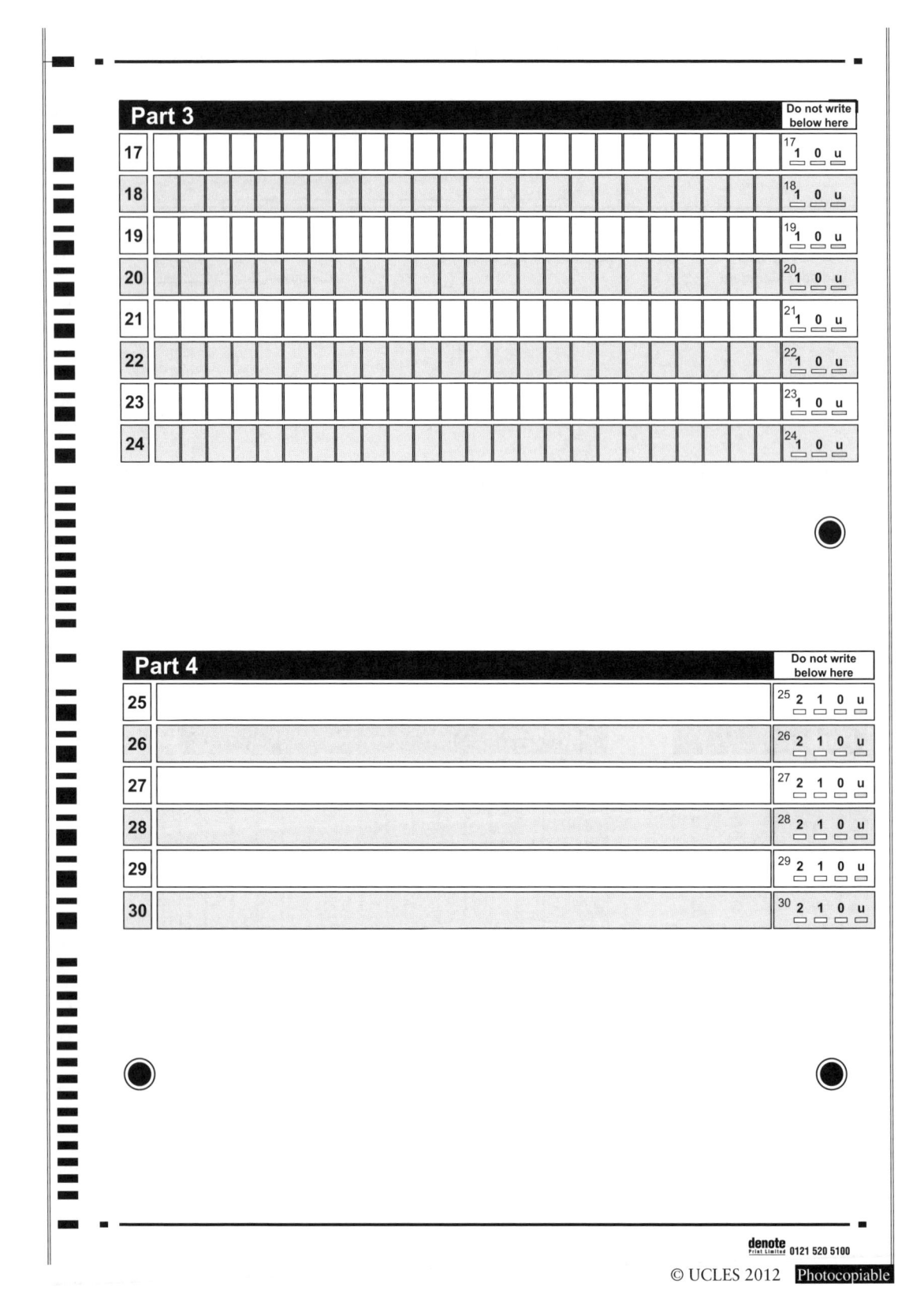

Part 3

17																
18																
19																
20																
21																
22																
23																
24																

Part 4

25	
26	
27	
28	
29	
30	

Sample answer sheet: Reading and Use of English

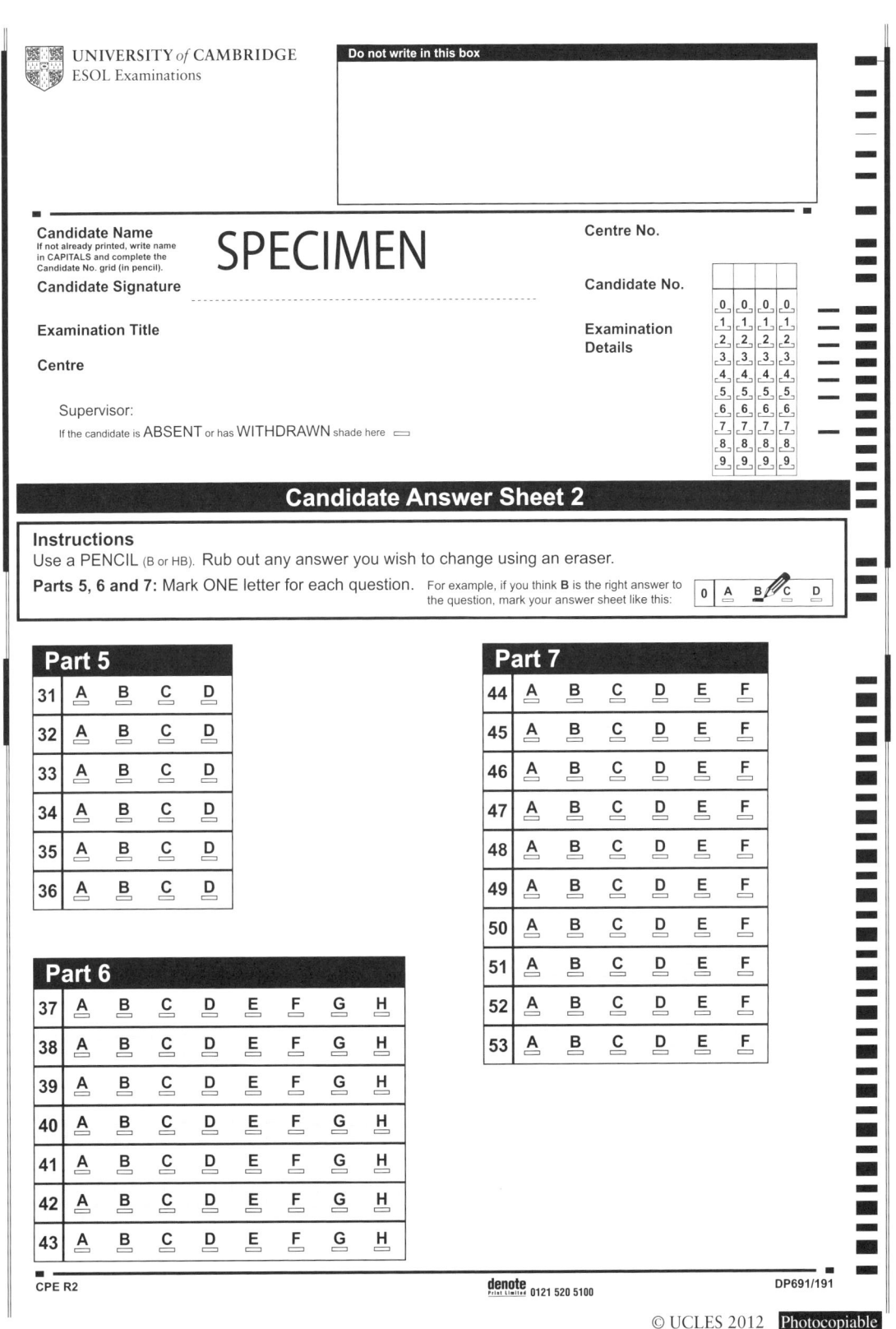

UNIVERSITY of CAMBRIDGE
ESOL Examinations

Do not write in this box

Candidate Name
If not already printed, write name in CAPITALS and complete the Candidate No. grid (in pencil).

Candidate Signature

Examination Title

Centre

Supervisor:
If the candidate is ABSENT or has WITHDRAWN shade here

SPECIMEN

Centre No.

Candidate No.

Examination Details

Candidate Answer Sheet 2

Instructions
Use a PENCIL (B or HB). Rub out any answer you wish to change using an eraser.
Parts 5, 6 and 7: Mark ONE letter for each question. For example, if you think **B** is the right answer to the question, mark your answer sheet like this: 0 A B C D

Part 5

31	A	B	C	D
32	A	B	C	D
33	A	B	C	D
34	A	B	C	D
35	A	B	C	D
36	A	B	C	D

Part 6

37	A	B	C	D	E	F	G	H
38	A	B	C	D	E	F	G	H
39	A	B	C	D	E	F	G	H
40	A	B	C	D	E	F	G	H
41	A	B	C	D	E	F	G	H
42	A	B	C	D	E	F	G	H
43	A	B	C	D	E	F	G	H

Part 7

44	A	B	C	D	E	F
45	A	B	C	D	E	F
46	A	B	C	D	E	F
47	A	B	C	D	E	F
48	A	B	C	D	E	F
49	A	B	C	D	E	F
50	A	B	C	D	E	F
51	A	B	C	D	E	F
52	A	B	C	D	E	F
53	A	B	C	D	E	F

CPE R2

© UCLES 2012 Photocopiable

Sample answer sheet: Listening

UNIVERSITY of CAMBRIDGE
ESOL Examinations

Do not write in this box

Candidate Name
If not already printed, write name in CAPITALS and complete the Candidate No. grid (in pencil).

SPECIMEN

Candidate Signature

Examination Title

Centre

Supervisor:
If the candidate is ABSENT or has WITHDRAWN shade here

Test version: A B C D E F J K L M N

Centre No.

Candidate No.

Examination Details

Special arrangements: S H

Candidate Answer Sheet

Instructions

Use a PENCIL (B or HB).
Rub out any answer you wish to change using an eraser.

Parts 1, 3 and 4:
Mark ONE letter for each question.

For example, if you think **B** is the right answer to the question, mark your answer sheet like this:

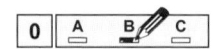

Part 2:
Write your answer clearly in CAPITAL LETTERS.

Write one letter or number in each box.
If the answer has more than one word, leave one box empty between words.

For example:

| 0 | N | U | M | B | E | R | | 1 | 2 | | | |

Turn this sheet over to start.

CPE L

DP692/192

© UCLES 2012 Photocopiable

Sample answer sheet: Listening

Part 1

1	A	B	C
2	A	B	C
3	A	B	C
4	A	B	C
5	A	B	C
6	A	B	C

Part 2 (Remember to write in CAPITAL LETTERS or numbers)

Do not write below here

7 — 1 0 u
8 — 1 0 u
9 — 1 0 u
10 — 1 0 u
11 — 1 0 u
12 — 1 0 u
13 — 1 0 u
14 — 1 0 u
15 — 1 0 u

Part 3

16	A	B	C	D
17	A	B	C	D
18	A	B	C	D
19	A	B	C	D
20	A	B	C	D

Part 4

21	A	B	C	D	E	F	G	H
22	A	B	C	D	E	F	G	H
23	A	B	C	D	E	F	G	H
24	A	B	C	D	E	F	G	H
25	A	B	C	D	E	F	G	H
26	A	B	C	D	E	F	G	H
27	A	B	C	D	E	F	G	H
28	A	B	C	D	E	F	G	H
29	A	B	C	D	E	F	G	H
30	A	B	C	D	E	F	G	H

denote Print Limited 0121 520 5100

© UCLES 2012 Photocopiable